The

Reference

Shelf

Campaign Finance Reform

Edited by Christopher Luna

The Reference Shelf
Volume 73 • Number 1

The H.W. Wilson Company
2001

The Reference Shelf

The books in this series contain reprints of articles, excerpts from books, addresses on current issues, and studies of social trends in the United States and other countries. There are six separately bound numbers in each volume, all of which are usually published in the same calendar year. Numbers one through five are each devoted to a single subject, providing background information and discussion from various points of view and concluding with a subject index and comprehensive bibliography that lists books, pamphlets, and abstracts of additional articles on the subject. The final number of each volume is a collection of recent speeches, and it contains a cumulative speaker index. Books in the series may be purchased individually or on subscription.

Library of Congress has cataloged this serial title as follows:

Campaign finance reform/ edited by Christopher Luna.
    p. cm.— (The reference shelf ; v. 73, no. 1)
    Includes bibliographical references and index.
    ISBN 0-8242-0998-2 (pbk)
       1. Campaign funds—United States—History. 2. Campaign funds—Law and legislation—United States—History. I. Luna, Christopher. II. Series.

JK1991 .C344 2001
324.7'8'0973—dc21   00-068568

Visit H.W. Wilson's Web site: www.hwwilson.com

Printed in the United States of America

Contents

Preface

Campaign spending has increased dramatically in recent years. During the 2000 election year, more than $3 billion were raised by national and local campaigns, and the two major parties spent record-breaking amounts on their presidential candidates. Although one may be tempted to characterize the steady decrease in the number of Americans who exercise their right to vote as evidence of an apathetic populace, many of those who abstain suffer instead from a sense of hopelessness in the face of widespread corruption in politics. There is a general perception that monied interests have acquired so much power to sway politicians that the concerns of individual citizens have been forgotten. This has led some to believe that their vote does not count.

Corporations have been prohibited from contributing to political campaigns since Congress passed the Tillman Act in 1907; nonetheless, those companies that support particular candidates have always been able to find ways around campaign finance regulations. Recently, unregulated donations known as soft money have created a loophole that allows wealthy individuals and corporations to spend many millions of dollars to influence legislation. Campaign finance regulations were instituted under President Richard Nixon in 1972, but following the Watergate scandal, it was learned that both parties had engaged in illegal fund-raising. The Federal Election Campaign Act (FECA) of 1974 set strict limits on campaign contributions and established the Federal Election Commission both to keep a record of donations and to enforce the new laws. In 1976 the United States Supreme Court weakened the effect of the FECA in *Buckley v. Valeo* by removing many of the contribution limits set forth by the law, and many corporations and political organizations quickly took advantage of their newfound freedom to spend.

Determining how donations affect policy is problematic, since in many cases, corporations contribute comparable amounts to both parties. Many efforts have been made to enact campaign finance reform in the wake of the 1996 election, a campaign which saw both parties accused of impropriety. But not everyone agrees that such efforts are necessary; opponents of reform maintain that limits on spending violate the spirit of the First Amendment. Not surprisingly, many of those opposed to campaign finance reform have been incumbent office holders who have historically benefitted from existing finance regulations. An important campaign finance reform bill co-sponsored by Senators John McCain and Russell Feingold was rejected by the Congress several years in a row.

The articles collected in this book explore many facets of this complex issue, beginning with an overview of the history of campaign finance practices, abuses, and regulations throughout U.S. history in Section I. The second section addresses the issue of the unregulated contributions known as soft money, a trend some see as necessary and others find hopelessly corrupt. Section III features both sides of the debate over campaign finance reform and includes a selection of articles written from particular perspectives. The fourth and final section looks at recent local and national efforts toward reform. The authors of the articles assembled here address several questions raised by the subject of campaign finance. For example, are politicians influenced by their contributors' agendas, and if so, to what extent do they return the favor in kind? Is money a form of political speech? Are the voices of citizens who are not affiliated with high-powered corporations or political organizations being heard by those within the power structure? What, if anything, can be done to restore honesty and integrity to United States politics? This book is intended to provide an evenhanded examination of these contentious issues.

The editor would like to thank the publishers and authors who granted permission for the use of their articles for this publication. This book would not have been possible without the patience and assistance of the following individuals: Gray Young, Sandra Watson, Jacquelene Latif, Lynn Messina, and Sara Yoo. I am very grateful to all of them for the hard work they contributed to the preparation of this volume.

Christopher Luna
January 2001

I. The History of Campaign Finance in the U.S.

Editor's Introduction

T he debate over campaign finance reform has been the subject of much discussion recently, especially in the four years since the 1996 presidential election. But campaign finance has generated heated debate in the United States since the late 19th Century. This section provides an overview of the history of campaign finance, as well as an introduction to many of the issues explored in greater depth throughout the book.

In "Money and Politics: A History of Campaign Finance Law," Anthony Corrado provides an account of campaign spending from William McKinley's first presidential campaign in the late 1880s to the scandals and reform measures of the last three decades. As Corrado points out, calls for reform came as early as 1905. This article describes the creation of important laws, such as the Federal Corrupt Practices Act of 1925 and the Federal Election Campaign Act of 1971, and takes a look at the strategies employed by political parties and candidates to exploit the loopholes in campaign finance regulation. These include the widespread use of "soft money," or contributions that are not limited by campaign finance law. The next article, "Money Troubles," is a special report by *Washington Post* reporter Dan Froomkin that examines the role of money in political campaigns and discusses the difficulty in curbing a system that thrives on financial donations.

The final two articles in this section look at the role of the Federal Election Commission (FEC), the organization established to monitor political contributions. In "Designed for Impotence," Joshua Wolf Shenk claims that the FEC was designed by Congress to be both weak and ineffective. He points out that the legislature, reluctant to enact true reform, structured the FEC to fail. Congress also has the power to withhold or cut funds from the commission, a situation which may effect the FEC's ability to adequately enforce campaign finance law. In the next article, "Scandal of the Past, Present and Future," Ellen Miller and Micah Sifry, senior analysts for the public interest group Public Campaign, discuss loopholes in campaign finance regulation, including soft money, a subject explored further in Section II.

A History of Federal Campaign Finance Law[1]

BY ANTHONY CORRADO
EXCERPTED FROM THE BOOK *CAMPAIGN FINANCE REFORM: A SOURCEBOOK*

Controversy over the role of money in politics did not begin with Watergate. Nor did it start with the clamor over the high costs of campaigning that accompanied the growth of radio and television broadcasting in the postwar era. Money's influence on the political process has long been a concern, an outgrowth of our nation's continuing struggle to reconcile basic notions of political equality, such as the principle of "one person, one vote," with the unequal distribution of economic resources and the willingness of a relatively small group of citizens to participate financially in political campaigns. Though public criticism of the campaign finance system has been particularly acute in recent decades, the criticisms raised, and the consequent demand for campaign finance reform, can be traced back to almost every election since at least the Civil War.

The first major thrust for campaign finance legislation at the national level came during the progressive era as a result of a movement to eliminate the influence of big business in federal elections. By the end of the nineteenth century, lavish contributions by major corporations and wealthy "fat cat" donors had reached levels that alarmed progressive reformers. Money from corporations, banks, railroads, and other businesses had become a major source of political funds, and numerous corporations were reportedly making donations to national party committees in amounts of $50,000 or more to "represent their share in the nation's prosperity. In the elections of 1896 and 1900, Mark Hanna relied on such corporate largesse to raise millions of dollars for William McKinley's presidential campaigns, most of which came from businesses or wealthy individuals with interests in government policy. Muckraking journalists and progressive politicians charged that these wealthy donors were corrupting government processes and gaining special favors and privileges as a result of their campaign gifts. They demanded regulation to prevent such abuses. Their calls

---

1. Introduction to Chapter 2, "Money and Politics," by Anthony Corrado, from *Campaign Finance Reform: A Sourcebook*, edited by Thomas E. Mann et al. Copyright © 1997 by The Brookings Institution. Reprinted with permission.

went unheeded until the controversy surrounding the financing of the 1904 election led to the first organized movement for campaign finance reform.

In 1904, Judge Alton B. Parker, the Democratic presidential nominee, alleged that corporations were providing President Theodore Roosevelt with campaign gifts to buy influence with the administration. Roosevelt denied the charge; but in investigations conducted after the election, several major companies admitted making large contributions to the Republican campaign. The controversy led Roosevelt to include a call for campaign finance reform in his annual messages to Congress in 1905 and 1906. This spurred the formation of the National Publicity Law Organization (NPLO), a citizens' group dedicated to lobbying for the regulation of political finance and public disclosure of political spending.

Controversy over the role of money in politics did not begin with Watergate.

Faced with increasing public sentiment in favor of reform, Congress finally acted in 1907. At the urging of Benjamin "Pitchfork Ben" Tillman, it took up a bill that had been introduced in an earlier Congress to restrict corporate giving in federal elections. The law, known as the Tillman Act, prohibited any contributions by corporations and national banks to federal political campaigns. This ban on corporate gifts to federal candidates remains in effect to this day, although it has been undermined in recent decades by the "soft (non-federal) money" fund-raising practices of national party committees.

Though the Tillman Act constituted a landmark in federal law, its adoption did not quell the cries for reform. Eliminating corporate influence was only one of the ideas being advanced at this time to clean up political finance. Reducing the influence of wealthy individuals was also a concern, and some reformers pushed for limits on individual donations. Still others advocated even bolder ideas. The NPLO continued to press for disclosure of party campaign receipts and expenditures so that voters could know which interests were financing which campaigns. William Bourke Cockran, a Democratic representative from New York associated with Tammany Hall, had an even more radical idea. In 1904 he suggested that the problems caused by campaign funding might be relieved if the government paid for some or all of the expenses of a presidential election. This proposal was never considered by Congress. However, in his December 1907 message to Congress, President Roosevelt did suggest the possibility of public financing for party organizations. But few legislators were willing to pursue this idea.

The continuing pressure for reform produced additional legislation a few years later. On the eve of the 1910 elections, the Republican majority in Congress passed a bill initiated by the NPLO that required party committees "operating in two or more states" to report any contributions or expenditures made in connection with campaigns for the House of Representatives. As adopted, the Federal Corrupt Practices Act, more commonly known as the Publicity Act of 1910, required nothing more than postelection reports of the receipts and expenditures of national party committees or committees operating in two or more states. Consequently, the act only affected the national party committees and their congressional campaign committees, and it did not require any disclosure prior to an election. Such a modest measure failed to appease the more vocal advocates of reform.

In the 1910 elections the Democrats took control of the House and picked up seats in the Senate. When the new Congress convened, the Democrats sought to revise the Publicity Act to include preelection reporting. House Republicans hoped to defeat the bill by adding provisions that would be unacceptable to Southern Democrats. Since Southerners favored states' rights and considered primaries the most important elections, House Republicans called for the regulation of committees operating in a single congressional district and the disclosure of primary campaign finances. Senate Republicans went even further, adopting a bill that included limits on campaign spending. But these tactics backfired; the Republican game of one-upmanship failed to defeat the bill. Instead, Congress ultimately agreed to reforms far more extensive than those originally proposed.

The 1911 Amendments to the Publicity Act improved disclosure and established the first spending limits for federal campaigns. The amendments extended disclosure in two ways. They required Senate as well as House campaigns to report receipts and expenditures. In addition, they required campaign committees to report their finances both before and after an election, in primary contests as well as general elections. The law also limited House campaign expenditures to a total of $5,000 and Senate campaign expenditures to $10,000 or the amount established by state law, whichever was less.

These spending limits quickly became controversial and were contested in court. Truman H. Newberry, a Michigan Republican who defeated Henry Ford in a fiercely contested Senate primary in 1918, was convicted of violating the spending limit in that race. His campaign committee reported spending close to $180,000 in its effort to secure the nomination, an amount almost 100 times the limit established by Michigan law. Newberry challenged the con-

viction, arguing that Congress had no authority to regulate primaries. Besides (the argument went), he and his codefendants had not
violated the law, which applied to campaign committees, not to the
candidate or individual supporters.

In 1921, the Supreme Court ruled in *Newberry v. United States*
(256 U.S. 232) that the congressional authority to regulate elections
did not extend to party primaries and nomination activities, thus
striking down the spending limits. This narrow interpretation of
congressional authority stood until 1941, when in *United States v.
Classic* (313 U.S. 299), the Court ruled that Congress did have the
authority to regulate primaries wherever state law made them part
of the election process and wherever they effectively determined the
outcome of the general election. But Congress did not reassert its
authority to regulate the financing of primary campaigns until
1971, when it adopted the Federal Election Campaign Act.

The Court's decision in *Newberry* was not the only event that high-
lighted the inadequacy of campaign finance reforms. Shortly after
this ruling, the Teapot Dome scandal once again drew attention to
the corruptive influence of large contributions. (In this case, the
scandal involved gifts made by oil developers in a nonelection year
to federal officials responsible for granting oil leases.) The scandal
led Congress to act once again, this time passing the Federal Corrupt Practices Act of 1925, which stood as the basic legislation governing campaign finance until the 1970s.

The Federal Corrupt Practices Act of 1925 essentially followed the
regulatory approach outlined by earlier legislation with little substantive change, except for the deletion of regulations governing primaries. The act revised the disclosure rules to account for the
financial activity that led to the Teapot Dome scandal by requiring
all multistate political committees (as well as House and Senate
candidates) to file quarterly reports that included all contributions
of $100 or more, even in nonelection years. The law also revised the
spending limits. Senate campaigns would be allowed to spend up to
$25,000 and House campaigns up to $5,000, unless state law called
for a lower limit.

Despite these changes, an effective regulatory regime was never
established. Though the law imposed clear reporting requirements,
it provided for none of the publicity or enforcement mechanisms
needed for meaningful disclosure. The law did not specify who
would have access to the reports; it did not require that they be published; it did not even stipulate the penalties if committees failed to
comply. As a result, many candidates did not file regular reports.
When they did, the information was provided in various forms.

Gaining access to the information through the Clerk of the House or Secretary of the Senate was difficult, and the reports were usually maintained for only two years and then destroyed.

The spending ceilings were even less effective and, in fact, were almost universally ignored. Because the limits were applicable to party committees, they were easily skirted by creating multiple committees for the same candidate or race. Each of these committees could then technically comply with the spending limit established for a particular race, while the total monies funneled into that race greatly exceeded the amount intended by the law. These multiple committees also facilitated evasion of disclosure. Donors

---

Congress did not return to the issue of campaign financing until the success of Franklin Roosevelt's New Deal coalition led conservative Democrats and staunch Republicans to seek additional reforms.

---

could provide gifts of less than $100 to each committee without any reporting obligation, or give larger amounts to a variety of committees, thus obscuring the total given to any candidate.

Wealthy donors also contributed monies through family members, and there were widespread reports of corporations providing bonuses to employees, who passed these funds on to candidates. Yet in the history of the 1925 act, no one was prosecuted for failing to comply with the law. Only two people—Republicans William S. Vare of Pennsylvania and Frank L. Smith of Virginia—were excluded from office for violating spending limits. And they were excluded in 1927 as a result of violations incurred in the first election in which the law was in place. Over the next forty-five years, no other candidates were punished under this act.

Even though it was well known that candidates and party committees were not complying with the dictates of federal law, Congress did not return to the issue of campaign financing until the success of Franklin Roosevelt's New Deal coalition led conservative Democrats and staunch Republicans to seek additional reforms. With the approach of the 1940 election, these opponents of Roosevelt's liberal politics became increasingly concerned that the rapidly expanding federal workforce that arose under the New Deal would become a permanent political force in the Democratic Party. In an attempt to minimize this possibility, Congress passed the Hatch Act of 1939, named after its sponsor, Senator Carl Hatch, a Democrat from New Mexico. The Hatch Act extended the prohibitions on political activity by federal employees that were first established when the Pendleton Civil Service Act of 1883 created the civil service system. The Pendleton Act sought to restrain the influence of the spoils system in the selection of civil service workers and to reduce the reliance of party organizations on the assessment of federal officeholders as a source of campaign revenue. The law prohibited government civil service employees from soliciting political contributions and protected federal officeholders from forced campaign assessments.

Although the "classified" offices covered under the original legislation covered only about one-tenth of the civil service, subsequent administrations expanded the coverage. The 1939 Hatch Act, which was also called the Clean Politics Act, prohibited political activity by those federal workers who were not constrained by the Pendleton Act. It also specifically prohibited federal employees from soliciting campaign contributions, which removed a major source of revenue for state and local party organizations.

In 1940, Congress passed amendments to the Hatch Act to restrict the amount of money donated to political campaigns in another way. The revisions imposed a limit of $5,000 per year on individual contributions to federal candidates or national party committees and of $3 million on the total amount that could be received or spent by a party committee operating in two or more states. Like earlier regulations, these restrictions had little effect on political giving. Donors could still donate large sums by giving to multiple committees or by making contributions through state and local party organizations, which were not subject to the $5,000 limit.

Another change in political finance during the New Deal era was the rise of labor unions as a major source of campaign money. Roosevelt's policies, many of which were regarded as pro-labor, encouraged union membership and led to the growth of organized labor as a political force in national politics. Union funds became an important source of Democratic Party campaign money. This financial strength grew significantly in the early 1940s with the establishment of the Political Action Committee as the political arm of the Congress of Industrial Organizations (CIO). Republicans and Southern Democrats sought to reduce labor's influence by passing the Smith-Connally Act, or War Labor Disputes Act of 1943. This act prohibited labor unions from using their treasury funds to make political contributions to candidates for federal office.

The Smith-Connally Act, which was passed over President Roosevelt's veto, was adopted as a war measure and thus automatically expired six months after the end of the war. When the Republicans recaptured Congress in 1946, they made this ban permanent by including it as one of the provisions of the Taft-Hartley Act, or the Labor Management Relations Act of 1947. This prohibition against the use of labor union treasury funds as a source of candidate contributions has been part of federal law ever since, matching the 1907 ban on corporate treasury funds.

In the decades after World War II, dramatic changes took place in the financing of political campaigns. Although party organizations remained an important source of revenue, campaigns became increasingly candidate based. Candidates for federal office established their own committees and raised funds independent of party efforts. At the same time, television was becoming an essential means of political communication, which significantly increased the costs of seeking federal office. Yet despite renewed concerns about the costs of campaigns and the role of wealth in national elections, Congress took no action. In fact, the only serious gesture made toward reform between World War II and the Vietnam War era was President John F. Kennedy's decision to form a Commission on Campaign Costs to explore problems in the system and develop legislative proposals. The Commission's 1962 report offered a comprehensive program of reform, including such innovative ideas as a system of public matching funds for presidential candidates. However, Congress was not receptive to the president's proposals, and no effort was made to resurrect these ideas after his assassination.

> *In the decades after World War II, dramatic changes took place in the financing of political campaigns.*

Congress did pass a related bill in 1966, but it never took effect. Campaign finance issues were once again in the news as a result of criticism of the Democratic "President's Club"—a group of donors, including some government contractors, who each gave $1,000 or more—and the censure of Senator Thomas Dodd (D–Conn.) for using his political funds for personal purposes.

Under the leadership of Senator Russell Long (D–La.), the powerful chair of the Senate Finance Committee, Congress passed the first major reform bill since 1925. Long hoped to reduce the potential influence of wealthy donors and ease the fund-raising demands generated by the rising costs of elections by providing public subsidies to political parties to pay the costs of the presidential campaign. These subsidies would be appropriated from a "Presidential Election Campaign Fund," which would be financed by allowing taxpayers to use a federal tax checkoff to allocate $1 for this purpose. The proposal met with widespread criticism, but Long forced the Senate to approve the unusual measure by attaching it as a rider to the Foreign Investors Tax Act.

Long's victory was short-lived. In the spring of 1967, Senator Albert Gore, a Democrat from Tennessee, and Senator John Williams, a Republican from Delaware, sponsored an amendment to repeal the Long Act. Gore favored public financing, arguing that the Long plan discriminated against third parties and would do little to control campaign costs, since it simply added public money to the private funds already being raised. Others simply opposed the idea of using government funds to finance campaigns or argued that such a system of party subsidies would place too much power into the hands of the national party leaders. Eventually, after much legislative maneuvering, Congress decided to make the Long Act inoperative by voting to postpone the checkoff until guidelines could be developed governing disbursement of any funds collected through this device.

Even if the Long Act had been implemented, it would not have addressed the major problems that had emerged in the campaign finance system. By this time, it was obvious to most observers that the reporting requirements and spending limits set forth in the Federal Corrupt Practices Act had proven wholly ineffective and needed a complete overhaul. There was also increasing concern about the rising costs of campaigns. In the 1956 elections, total campaign spending was approximately $155 million, $9.8 million of which was used for radio and television advertising. By 1968, overall spending had nearly doubled to $300 million, while media expenditures had increased by almost 600 percent to $58.9 million.

This dramatic growth worried many members of Congress, who feared that they might be unable to raise the sums needed in future campaigns if costs kept escalating. Legislators also worried about wealthy challengers who might have access to the resources needed to defeat them in expensive media-based campaigns. Democrats were particularly concerned about the rising costs, since Republicans had demonstrated greater success at raising large sums and had spent more than twice as much as the Democrats in the 1968 presidential contest. Changing patterns of political finance thus sparked interest in further reform, and Congress responded by passing the Federal Election Campaign Act of 1972.

The Federal Election Campaign Act (FECA) went into effect in 1972. It restricted rising campaign costs and strengthened national reporting and disclosure requirements. The legislation sought to address problems stemming from the Federal Corrupt Practices Act and cut rising campaign costs, thereby combining two approaches to reform. The first part of the law established contribution limits on the amount a candidate could give to his or her own campaign, and set ceilings on the amount a campaign could spend on media. The second part imposed strict public disclosure procedures on federal candidates and political committees.

The FECA represented a departure from previous regulatory efforts by placing specific limits on the amounts candidates could spend on media advertising in both primaries and general elections. These limits may have helped to restrict media spending in 1972 but did little to slow the increase in campaign spending. The information gathered as a result of the new disclosure requirements revealed that total campaign expenses rose from an estimated $300 million in 1968 to $425 million in 1972. The growth in presidential campaign costs was especially significant: President Richard M. Nixon spent more than twice as much in 1972 as he did

---

The FECA Amendments of 1974 represent the most comprehensive campaign finance legislation ever adopted.

---

in 1968, while his Democratic opponent in 1972, George McGovern, spent more than four times what Hubert Humphrey did in 1968— and was still outspent by a substantial margin. These spending patterns suggested that more extensive expenditure limits would be needed if costs were to be brought under control. But before the new law could be tested in another election, the Watergate scandal broke and a more extensive system of regulation was adopted.

In 1974 Congress thoroughly revised the federal campaign finance system in response to the pressure for comprehensive reform in the wake of Watergate and other reports of financial abuse in the 1972 Nixon campaign. Detailed investigations into the Nixon campaign revealed an alarming reliance on large contributions, illegal corporate contributions, and undisclosed slush funds. They also raised questions about money's influence on the political process—it was alleged that contributors "bought" ambassadorships, gained special legislative favors, and enjoyed other special privileges. The scandals spurred Congress to change the law once again.

The FECA Amendments of 1974 represent the most comprehensive campaign finance legislation ever adopted. Although technically a set of amendments to the 1971 law, the 1974 act left few of the original provisions intact. It significantly strengthened the disclosure provisions of the 1971 law and enacted unprecedented limits on contributions and expenditures in federal elections. The law set specific limits on the amounts individuals, political committees, and party organizations could donate to federal campaigns. It also replaced the media expenditure ceilings adopted two years earlier with aggregate spending ceilings for presidential, senatorial, and congressional candidates. Limits on the amounts party organizations could spend on behalf of federal candidates were also established. To administer and enforce these provisions, the act created an independent agency, the Federal Election Commission (FEC), which was given primary authority for regulating political finance.

The most innovative aspect of the 1974 law was the creation of an optional program of full public financing for presidential general election campaigns and a voluntary system of public matching subsidies for presidential primary campaigns. As a result, it introduced the first program of public campaign funding at the national level. In general election campaigns, the presidential nominees for the major parties could receive an amount equal to the aggregate spending limit if they agreed to refrain from raising any additional private money. Qualified minor party or independent candidates could receive a proportional share of the subsidy. In prenomination campaigns, the candidates could qualify for matching subsidies on small contributions. The purpose was to reduce fund-raising pressures in national contests and encourage solicitation of small donations. The funding for this program came from a voluntary tax checkoff on federal income tax forms—funds deposited in the Presidential Election Campaign Fund, a separate account maintained by the U.S. Treasury.

This tax checkoff mechanism originated with the Revenue Act of 1971, the successor to Long's 1966 proposal, which laid the foundation for a less comprehensive system of public subsidies for presidential campaigns. This subsidy program had not yet been implemented when the 1974 legislation was passed. To avoid a threatened veto by President Nixon, Congress had to postpone any collection of revenues until 1973 for funds to be used in the 1976 election.

Another important feature of the Revenue Act was the creation of a federal income tax credit or tax deduction for small contributions to political candidates at all levels of government and to some political committees, including those associated with national party organizations. Like the matching funds program at the presidential level, this provision was designed to promote broad-based participation in elections. This tax benefit was modified by the Revenue Act of 1978, which eliminated the tax deduction option and doubled the maximum allowable tax credit. This credit was available until 1986, when it was repealed by the Tax Reform Act of 1986.

Like its 1971 predecessor, the 1974 law was substantially revised before it was ever fully implemented. As a result of the Supreme Court's findings in *Buckley v. Valeo* (424 U.S. 1 [1976]), Congress was forced to adopt additional amendments in the midst of the 1976 primary elections. Most important, the Court ruled against the spending limits established for House and Senate candidates and the contribution limit for independent expenditures. This substantially weakened the potential efficacy of the act, because the only spending ceilings allowed to stand were those for publicly funded presidential campaigns. The Court also struck down the method of appointing Federal Election Commissioners. The 1976 amendments thus revised the means of appointing members of the Commission and made other changes in the public financing program, contribution limits, and disclosure procedures. But the law was not completed until May. This forced a two-month suspension of the public matching funds program, because the FEC was not allowed to exercise its powers until it was reconstituted in conformance with the Court's ruling.

Despite its shaky start, the new campaign finance system represented a major advancement over the patchwork of regulations it replaced. The disclosure and reporting requirements dramatically improved public access to financial information and regulators' ability to enforce the law. The contribution ceilings eliminated the large gifts that had tainted the process in 1972. Public financing quickly gained widespread acceptance among the candidates, and small contributions became a staple of presidential campaign financing.

But the new regime was not without its critics. Candidates and political committee operatives complained that the law's detailed reporting requirements forced them to engage in unnecessary and burdensome paperwork, which increased their administrative costs. State and local party leaders contended that the law reduced the level of spending on traditional party-building activities (such as voter registration and mobilization programs) and discouraged grass-roots volunteer efforts. Parties were limited in the amounts they could spend on behalf of candidates, and both presidential campaigns had chosen to concentrate their legally limited resources on media advertising rather than grass-roots political activities.

As a result of the initial experience with the FECA, Congress adopted additional revisions before the 1980 election. To ensure their quick passage, the Federal Election Campaign Act Amendments of 1979 centered on "noncontroversial" reforms acceptable to both houses of Congress. The 1979 law was thus designed primarily to revise the reporting and disclosure requirements, easing the paperwork required by participants and reducing the amount of financial information to be reported. But it also sought to address the concerns raised by state and local party officials regarding the diminished role of local party organizations in national elections. To this end, the 1979 law granted party organizations a limited exemption from the spending provisions of the 1976 act and allowed them to spend "federal" funds on certain grass-roots volunteer activities and on traditional activities such as voter registration and get-out-the-vote programs.

Although the parties still had to abide by the law's restrictions when raising these funds, the exemption from spending limits gave the local and state parties a much larger role in campaigns. This was especially so in Senate and presidential campaigns, where the parties are more likely to engage in such supplemental campaign

---

By the end of the 1980s, soft money funding had become a major component of national election financing, with both major national parties spending tens of millions of soft dollars.

---

activity. This exemption was designed to encourage volunteer activities and promote civic participation in the election process. Contrary to what is commonly believed, the 1979 amendments did not create soft money. They only allowed party committees to use "hard" dollars to fund certain narrowly specified activities for volunteers and for party-building purposes, without having those expenditures count against the party's contribution limitations to candidates.

With a "final" regulatory regime now in place, candidates and party organizations soon began to adapt to the new rules in ways both intended and unintended. Many of these responses undermined the efficacy of the regulations and raised further questions about the FECA's ability to control the flow of political money. Congressional campaign costs continued to rise, renewing concerns about the role money plays in federal races and how well challengers can compete financially against entrenched incumbents. Contributions and spending by political action committees (PACs) also became a big issue as the number of these committees increased and their resources were distributed in ways that provided substantial financial advantages to incumbents. At the presidential level, candidates and party organizations looked for ways of circumventing the expenditure and contribution limits that accompanied public funding.

Most noteworthy among these new tactics was the aggressive exploitation of the exemption for party-related activities, and the rise of a phenomenon known as soft money. Soft money is the common name given to party funds that are not regulated by federal law, but which the FEC has voted, through the Advisory Opinion process, to allow party committees to accept and spend on administrative expenses and for other allegedly non-federal election-related purposes.

By the end of the 1980s, soft money funding had become a major component of national election financing, with both major national parties spending tens of millions of soft dollars. Most of this money was being raised through unlimited contributions from sources such as corporations and labor unions that had long been banned from participating in federal elections. Many critics therefore argued that the FECA had failed and that the FEC was incapable of fulfilling its responsibility to enforce the law. Soft money is not a result of Congress's deliberation and action through the lawmaking process. Instead it is an almost inadvertent result of several FEC advisory opinions—approved without hearings, public comment, or much apparent thought for the enormous consequences for the federal campaign finance structure.

By 1986, Congress was once again confronting the issue of campaign finance reform. Although both houses of Congress have considered a number of different bills since 1986 and passed some version of reform on a couple of occasions, no new legislation has been adopted since 1979. Though there is consensus that the FECA is no longer working, there is wide disagreement as to how the problems should be fixed. Disagreements over the desirability and potential effects of such proposals as spending limits in House and Senate races, public subsidies at the congressional level, restrictions on PAC contributions, and the most effective means of eliminating soft money have produced more heat than light, often resulting in partisan gridlock or unresolvable differences between the upper and lower chambers of Congress.

History suggests that the best prospects for reform are when a new Congress faces some major financial controversy or scandal that has taken place in the previous election. The 105th Congress thus offers a new hope for reform. The unprecedented financial activities of 1996 have clearly demonstrated that the current regulatory scheme is broken; the allegations of illegal and improper fund-raising at the national level have created the most notable controversy since the Watergate scandal twenty-five years ago. Whether this will produce a new system of regulation or further innovation in campaign funding remains to be seen. Regardless of what happens, history suggests that questions concerning the role of money and politics will continue to be a regularly recurring feature of our nation's political landscape.

Money Troubles[2]

By Dan Froomkin
Washington Post, September 4, 1998

Campaign finance is a confusing topic in many ways. But it is money which, arguably, determines the very basics of our democracy: Who runs, who wins, and how they govern.

This overview summarizes the critical issues underlying the debate and the ongoing criminal investigations.

Part 1: Big Money—The Cost of Winning

The amount of money needed to win a federal election these days —most notably, the presidency—is enormous. The Clinton and Dole campaigns spent about $232 million in the 1996 campaign cycle— supplemented by about $69 million in "issue ads" paid for by the Republican and Democratic national committees. Across the country, Election '96 cost about $2.7 billion, the costliest ever.

It takes money to pay a campaign staff and buy materials. It takes money for a campaign to be taken seriously by the press. It even takes money to raise more money.

Perhaps more than anything, it takes an awful lot of money to buy television and radio ads—which are virtually mandatory for any national political campaign and for many local and statewide ones as well.

For example, a massive television advertising blitz that started in October 1995 greatly contributed to the Clinton reelection victory by retuning his image and drowning out any competing message. It didn't come cheap. The ads—which were paid for by the Democratic National Committee, not by the Clinton/Gore campaign—cost about $44 million.

In congressional campaigns, the amounts are smaller, but money generally plays a huge role. Big coffers scare away challengers; advertising can swing races. As a result, members of Congress spend a lot of time and energy—and money—raising funds for their next election.

Overview, Part 2: The Issues—What's for Sale?

So how do you raise the big money if you're running for office? What do you sell? And who are the buyers?

Ideally, the only commodity in the political marketplace is ideas. The best ideas are what sell, the consumers are the voters, and they make their selections in the voting booth.

But the reality of modern politics is that access and attention, if not policy, are for sale. Alliances with the wealthy are easy to make and painful to break. Independence and virtue are hard to maintain.

The question of just how much politicians sell their support has a certain chicken-and-egg quality to it. Over the years, Congress has given billions in tax breaks to industries and interest groups that contribute heavily to parties and campaigns. But does the money beget a vote? Or does a voting record beget the money?

"Members are only human," former representative and onetime Ways and Means Committee Chairman Sam Gibbons (D-Fla.) told *The Washington Post.* "You can't entirely disassociate yourself from something like a campaign contribution.

Average Cost of Winning a Seat in Congress, 1996	
Senate	$3,765,000
House	$675,000

How much it impacts on you and how far you're willing to move from your own principles is something each member has to decide for himself."

Major donors to the Democratic National Committee in 1996 were literally able to buy time with the president—one of the most rare and valuable resources in Washington. Does that kind of access give donors an unfair ability to affect administration policies and regulations?

To whatever extent politicians give access or policy considerations to donors, the people and interests being catered to inevitably have one thing in common: Money.

That in and of itself is offensive to some campaign finance reform groups, who think moneyed interests hold too much sway in the political world, at the expense of the poor—and they argue for strict limits on campaign spending and fund-raising.

But in the view of many Republicans, the Supreme Court and many civil libertarians, preventing someone from spending money to express their views unconstitutionally limits the right to free speech.

Another question: Is the amount of money spent on campaigns really excessive? Some say no. The entire amount spent on elections in 1996 is slightly less than the $2.8 billion that Phillip Morris spent on advertising in 1995.

Overview, Part 3: The Past Reforms—A Look at the Laws

Campaign finance rules were dramatically overhauled in the 1970s. The first major set of reforms was signed into law in early 1972 by Richard Nixon—whose reelection committee then went on to funnel illegal corporate contributions into slush funds, pay for break-ins and trade cash for favors. After the Watergate hearings, campaign laws were toughened once again.

The Federal Election Campaign Act amendments of 1974:

- Established strict disclosure requirements for campaign donations;
- Set specific limits for those donations;
- Instituted public financing of presidential elections;
- And established the Federal Election Commission (FEC) to be the campaign police.

The public financing of presidential elections, first administered in 1976, remains controversial—and widely misunderstood. The basic idea is that it's worth spending tax dollars to replace a system that encourages the unchecked solicitation of private money.

Here's how it works: Fueled by the voluntary checkoff on tax forms (now $3), the Presidential Election Campaign Fund matches up to $250 of each contribution made to eligible primary candidates. In return, the candidates must promise that they will limit spending to a certain amount and follow certain other rules. Then, in the general election season, the presidential candidates receive a lump sum in return for not accepting any further private donations.

In 1996, for example, the Clinton and Dole campaigns each received about $75 million in taxpayer money after promising not to spend more than $111 million (with a few exemptions).

Contribution Limits				
	To a candidate or candidate committee per primary or general election	To a national party committee per year	To any other political committee per year	Total per calendar year
Individuals	$1,000	$20,000	$5,000	$25,000
PACs	$5,000	$15,000	$5,000	No limit

The 1974 legislation also established contribution limits and rules about disclosure remain that remain in effect to this day. For instance, campaigns must name all contributors who donate more than $200 in a year.

Two major parts of the 1974 legislation were struck down by the Supreme Court. The post-Watergate amendments had also established mandatory spending limits—restricting total spending for all federal races, and even limiting independent spending on behalf of federal candidates.

Those provisions were struck down in the 1976 *Buckley v. Valeo* decision, in which the court ruled that they violated the First Amendment. The court also struck down a provision that would have limited how much money a candidate can contribute to his or her own campaign.

But by and large, the reforms seemed to be doing what they were intended to do.

For a while.

Overview, Part 4: Soft Money—A Look at the Loopholes

Over time, the politicians and special interests found ways around the rules.

Federal election law, especially after a 1979 amendment, allows political parties to spend as much as they want as long as the money goes to "party building activities," such as "get-out-the-vote" efforts and generic advertising, such as "issue" ads.

This spending is called "soft money." Unlike "hard money," with its firm limits on contributions, soft money is largely unregulated. There is, in fact, no limit whatsoever on the amount donors can give to a party as long as it goes into soft money accounts.

The parties raised small amounts of soft money through the '80s and early '90s. Then, during the 1996 campaign, the amounts skyrocketed. The two major parties raised more than $262 million in soft money—three times more than in 1992.

A June 1996 Supreme Court ruling contributed somewhat, by explicitly allowing political parties to spend as much as they want on congressional races as long as they act "independently" of the candidates.

But the boom in soft money was mostly a function of the vastly increased imagination with which the parties spent it. Much of the soft money raised by the national committees in 1996—about $120 million—was spent on "issue ads," theoretically supporting party positions, rather than specific candidates.

Both parties violated the spirit, if not the letter, of the law. Starting in late 1995, the Democratic National Committee used soft money to pay for a months-long blitz of television commercials, basically indistinguishable from campaign ads, that bolstered Clinton in the polls.

The Republican National Committee at one point spent soft money on a 60-second commercial crafted by Dole's advertising team with footage originally shot for the Dole campaign. The ad devoted 56 seconds to Dole's biography and four seconds to the issues.

Essentially, soft money blew a hole through the reforms of the 1970s. By any reasonable interpretation, the campaigns no longer adhered to contribution or spending limits. They voraciously courted private donors—the only difference being that money was sent to party committees, rather than their own campaign coffers. And the presidential campaigns still got their public financing.

In a similar vein, unions and other interest groups were able to spend about $70 million for political purposes—much of it on candidate-specific advertising—without adhering to public disclosure requirements. Because their ads, too, were supposedly designed to address issues, the origin and amount of cash they spent did not have to be reported to the FEC. And the groups didn't have to finance the ads from their political action committees, which, by law, could accept no more than $5,000 from any one source.

Much was written about the power of political action committees, or PACs, in the 1980s. Leveraging contributions from many individuals or companies, PACs could exert enormous clout. Their contributions, however, were limited to $5,000 per candidate, or $15,000 per national party committee.

Those numbers seem almost quaint compared to the soft money figures. Cumulatively, PACs still contributed about $218 million to federal campaigns in 1996. But in 1996, individuals or corporations that wanted to influence an election could donate hundreds of thousands of dollars to a party committee. Unions could do much more than just chip in $5,000 from a PAC. They could spend hundreds of thousands of dollars on "issue" advertising targeting or supporting a specific candidate—without any reporting requirement.

Overview, Part 5: Allegations—The Excesses of '96

With the contribution and spending caps now irrelevant, the vast appetite for money in the 1996 campaign led to excesses. And while the problem was bipartisan in nature, it is the Democratic National Committee and the White House that have been linked to the most outrageous conduct.

The DNC has acknowledged that many 1996 soft-money contributions were illegal or inappropriate, and has returned $2.8 million in contributions it identified, after the fact, as being from questionable sources—mostly foreign nationals or people contributing on behalf of third parties.

And the Clinton administration engaged in fund-raising tactics that, while not necessarily illegal, were widely perceived as unethical and tacky. With Clinton's explicit approval, donors were invited to spend the night in the White House's Lincoln Bedroom, or to meet with the president over coffee. A number of donors with

---

With the contribution and spending caps now irrelevant, the vast appetite for money in the 1996 campaign led to excesses.

---

questionable backgrounds swept into the White House without adequate security checks. Some even tried to take advantage of their access to the president to pursue personal financial opportunities.

The drive for cash also led to a blurring of the boundaries between government business and campaign business. For instance, Vice President Al Gore reportedly spoke by telephone with dozens of people from his White House office, each time seeking large contributions to the Democratic National Committee. Federal law generally bans government employees from raising campaign cash from federal property.

Once again, as in the 1972 Nixon campaign, donors were directly rewarded with favors from the White House—although just how far that parallel extends remains the subject of debate.

Those who looked to the Federal Election Commission to stop the excesses of '96 were sorely disappointed.

Since its founding, the commission has time and time again proved to be weak, slow and largely ineffective. Structured to deadlock—with three commissioners from each party—the FEC has also seen its budget and authority dwindle over time thanks to Congress and the courts.

As usual, it took no significant action.

Overview, Part 6: Legislation—Today's Reform Proposals

The public and party leaders agree that once again something needs to be done about campaign finance. But historically, the consensus has disintegrated whenever it came to specific proposals.

That's because the major parties take starkly different views on the specifics of the various "reform" proposals, largely depending on what the likely effect is on their bottom lines.

Democrats generally support limits in soft money and spending because of the GOP's traditional ability to raise funds from the wealthy. And while there is dissension in the ranks, Republicans generally argue against limits—particularly if unions remain unfettered in their spending of dues. Some Republican leaders support raising the current limits for individual contributions, which they say would reduce the time and energy spent on fund-raising.

Promises are made then broken. Deadlines are set then ignored. Clinton and House Majority Leader Newt Gingrich (R-Ga.) famously shook hands before a group of senior citizens in Claremont, N.H., in June 1995 and pledged to create a bipartisan commission to reform campaign finance. Nothing came of it.

But now prospects are looking less bleak. In February, one key bill won the support of a majority of senators before being filibustered to death by Republican leaders.

In April, in the face of a bipartisan rebellion, House Republican leaders reversed course and agreed to let campaign finance legislation come up for a vote.

And in early August, the House passed a far-reaching proposal co-sponsored by Republican Rep. Chris Shays of Connecticut and Democratic Rep. Martin Meehan of Massachusetts. Shays-Meehan is the House counterpart of the McCain-Feingold bill, the creation of Republican Sen. John McCain of Arizona and Democratic Sen. Russ Feingold of Wisconsin.

Shays-Meehan, much like McCain-Feingold, would:

- Bar state as well as national parties from raising or spending soft money. Instead, all contributions would be subject to limits that now apply to hard money.

- Prevent soft money from being rechanneled into independent expenditures by drawing a line between issue advocacy and outright advocacy of a particular candidate, including a ban on using a candidate's name or likeness within 60 days of an election.

- Require expanded and speedier disclosure of contributions and expenditures, including electronic filing, and impose stronger penalties for violations.

Democrats strongly back the bill. And the House vote, in which 61 Republicans defied their own leadership's attempts to derail the bill, puts enormous pressure on Senate Republicans to approve the plan. But the legislation is not likely to go any further before the 105th Congress adjourns in early October.

Any attempt to establish mandatory spending limits would likely run afoul of the Supreme Court's *Buckley v. Valeo* ruling. In March 1997, Sens. Ernest F. Hollings (D-S.C.) and Arlen Specter (R-Pa.) proposed a constitutional amendment to allow Congress to set such limits, but it was overwhelmingly voted down.

In the meantime, fund-raising proceeds at a record pace: The two political parties raised about $74 million in soft money during 1997 —more than twice the amount they raised during the comparable period four years earlier.

Ultimately, supporters of campaign finance reform face a paradox: Expecting people who live and die by money to actually regulate it. Nothing could be more political.

Designed for Impotence[3]

Why the Federal Election Commission Is a Lap Dog for the Political Class

By Joshua Wolf Shenk
U.S. News and World Report, January 20, 1997

The mouth-watering tip came anonymously to the Federal Election Commission in 1975: It accused Charlie Rose, a congressman from North Carolina, of greasing a local pol with a brand-new Cadillac. The newly created FEC looked into the charge and found it baseless, but that wasn't the end of the affair.

Rose's colleagues were furious that the agency had even looked. "If you don't fire the employees involved," thundered Wayne Hays, a powerful House member, to the FEC's chairman, "I'll cut the guts out of your budget. You've got some bums down there you've either got to fire or you'll be out of business." The threats were more than bluster. Congress sliced the FEC's 1976 budget request by 25 percent. To avoid another Rose-like inquiry, it banned the commission from following up tips that weren't signed and notarized. It was the first of many hostile reactions that the FEC provoked by trying to do its job.

Congress created the FEC to enforce the Federal Election Campaign Act of 1974. Today that law—and the FEC itself—seem woefully inadequate. Neither was a deterrent to illegal and irregular contributions to Democrats from convicted drug dealers and foreign arms merchants. As Republicans prepare separate House and Senate probes, the inadequacies of the FEC as a campaign watchdog will be laid bare in coming months. But it's not as if these problems are new. They have been plain for years.

Americans now think of campaign finance as institutionalized corruption. It is the rare politician who can win or hold office without selling access and influence. The Federal Election Commission isn't the prime culprit—that role is filled by lobbies that expect a return on their donations and politicians who shake them down. But the FEC's story is crucial to explaining how the system developed—and why it will be difficult to change.

Toothless. When it comes to disclosing how much politicians spend and raise, and from whom, the FEC works quickly and efficiently. Its data form the basis for most of what the public knows about campaign finance. The Democrats' "Asiagate" scandals, for example, began with an FEC list of party donors. Beyond collecting information, the agency makes it public via press releases, online databases and a reference room in Washington.

But the FEC is much less successful in its role as a campaign cop—sniffing out and punishing candidates who break the law. Campaigns routinely exceed spending limits and accept illegal money, knowing that any FEC punishment would be mild (only fines—no jail terms) and very slow in coming.

The agency's torpor is legendary in political circles. Last August, it dismissed charges that Pat Robertson's 1988 presidential campaign had improperly accepted $1.7 million in free air travel from the Christian Broadcasting Network. Weakness in the evidence was not the problem. The FEC concluded that the charges would be thrown out of court as too old.

The FEC isn't lazy or inept (the staff is esteemed). It is hampered by its very design. The agency was born of embarrassment, at a time when exposure of slush funds, corporate donations and pay-offs in the Nixon administration had cast a pall over the whole federal government.

But, while creating the illusion of reform, Congress made the FEC too weak to enforce the law. The agency can't conduct random audits or issue injunctions to stop violations in progress. Starting even a small investigation requires the votes of four of the FEC's six commissioners, as does every step in an inquiry. Defendants can appeal at every turn. If the agency finds a violation, even then its hands are tied: For 30 days the law requires the FEC to ask nicely for a fine, using "informal methods of conference, conciliation, and persuasion."

Delay, delay. To enforce a penalty, the agency has to take a violator to court—and endure more delays. The sanction against the campaign of former President George Bush for allegedly accepting $223,000 in illegal contributions in 1988 was a letter asking that his lawyers "take steps that this kind of activity does not occur in the future." The letter came nearly three years after Bush left office.

For any campaign, there is an incentive to drag out the process. After all, even if a fine is levied, the infraction will seem like a distant memory to the public. And candidates know that the watchdog has only gums. "It has no teeth, it's slow and it's cumbersome," says an aide to a top Republican senator. "And members like it that way."

When the FEC gets too tough, members have a way of striking back. For example, Congress outlawed the use of campaign funds for personal items—country club memberships, designer clothes and the like. But when the FEC wrote rules implementing the restrictions, the same Congress was outraged. The House rescinded nearly $3 million in already appropriated funds. And House Appropriations Chairman Bob Livingston sent a team of investigators to comb through the FEC for weeks, looking for areas to cut even deeper.

An excess of funds, however, has never been the FEC's problem. Its fiscal 1997 budget is $28.16 million, nearly a tenth of which is reserved for upgrading computers. Considering the amount of campaign cash the agency is chartered to keep track of—an estimated $2 billion was spent on the 1996 elections, compared with a real $800 million in 1976—its budget seems paltry. The independent counsels investigating the Clinton administration alone had spent more than $25 million as of the end of March 1996.

"Over the years," says Tony Coelho, a former Democratic representative and formidable fund-raiser, "there's basically been an attempt on the part of people to try to make the FEC noneffective by withholding money. And they succeeded to a great extent." The staff is bone thin: The FEC has only two investigators to cover its thousands of cases; its lawyers are saddled with as many as a dozen cases each. The most important work rarely receives the attention it requires.

The FEC's leadership structure is a cozy deal, too. Congress controls who becomes a commissioner: The president merely rubber-stamps recommendations from Capitol Hill. That means commissioners owe their $115,700-a-year jobs to party machinery. When the regulated control the regulators, oversight goes soft.

Consider Vice Chairman Joan Aikens, once an active Republican in Pennsylvania state politics. Asked if she thinks there is a money-in-politics problem, Aikens says, "I think there is a *perception* of a money-in-politics problem—put forth by the press and [by] agencies like Common Cause and the Center for Responsive Politics." Aikens also observes, "It seems to me that we ought to spend enough money to get good people elected . . . and if that takes $13 million for a Sen-

---

MONEY BAGS: "In the last campaign, people essentially did whatever they wanted, because they knew they'd get away with it. Millions of dollars were changing hands, and the FEC couldn't and wouldn't do anything."

Don Simon, executive vice president, Common Cause

ate candidate, then so be it." Aikens's logic is peculiar. High-cost campaigns lead to mudfests more often than to enlightened debate. And the more money that must be raised, the more potential there is for corruption.

The Democrats on the commission often favor stricter regulation than do Aikens and her fellow Republican Lee Ann Elliot, who came to the FEC from the American Medical Association's political action committee. But partisan splits have prevented action on a number of high-profile cases. No more than three commissioners can belong to one party, so it's impossible to muster a majority without winning a vote from the other side. Three Democrats, but no Republicans, voted to pursue a case against the National

> ## *The most basic challenge to the FEC, and to election regulations as a whole, has come from the federal courts.*

Republican Senatorial Committee for overspending in the 1988 campaign of Sen. Conrad Burns of Montana. Three Republicans, but no Democrats, voted to rescind a full $4.1 million in public funds from Clinton's 1992 campaign. Ironically, the highest-profile cases are the least likely to receive action. Former Clinton consultant Dick Morris has confirmed that President Clinton and his advisers coordinated commercials paid for by the Democratic National Committee—an apparent violation of the law. But few expect the FEC to follow up.

Finding four votes to take action has been especially difficult since October 1995, when Republican commissioner Trevor Potter stepped down. Potter was acclaimed for his aggressiveness; he helped launch regulations against personal use by politicians of campaign funds and pushed for a lawsuit against Newt Gingrich's GOPAC for supporting federal candidates (including Gingrich) when it wasn't registered to do so. But Potter quit in frustration after ideas he favored repeatedly failed to become policy. Meanwhile, Congress and President Clinton have yet to name a successor and the chance of getting four votes for any enforcement action is further reduced.

Court clash. The FEC has enough trouble with congressmen undermining their own laws, commissioners who don't believe there is a money-in-politics problem, and a process that is painfully slow to fill empty seats on the commission. But the most basic challenge to the FEC, and to election regulations as a whole, has come from the federal courts. While the law was still in its infancy, the Supreme Court, in *Buckley v. Valeo*, voided large chunks of it in

1976. The ruling declared that a limit on campaign spending is equivalent to a limit on free speech, and it laid the basis for decades of rulings against FEC restrictions that would have reined in (and forced disclosure of) both spending and giving.

Since then, courts have relentlessly nipped away at the agency's already limited authority. Take the AFL-CIO's $35 million advertising barrage in 1996. Because it disparaged specific Republican candidates, advanced the agenda of their Democratic opponents and peaked right before Election Day, you might expect that spending for the ads would be considered campaign spending and therefore subject to FEC rules.

But under *Buckley,* the FEC can act only if the ads expressly advocate a candidate's election or defeat. And in a series of subsequent cases, the label "express advocacy" has been limited to material that uses a list of obvious phrases (such as "vote for" or "vote against"). In 1994, for example, a federal trial court in New York found that a mass mailing asking readers to return a "special election-year ANTI-WAR ballot" with "your No vote for President Reagan" could not be considered express advocacy.

One court, the 9th Circuit Court of Appeals, has run against the vein. It defined express advocacy as something a reasonable person would see as pushing for a candidate's election or defeat. But the Supreme Court is moving in the opposite direction. In a ruling last summer, four justices signaled their interest in repealing restrictions altogether. That decision, *Colorado Republican Federal Campaign Committee v. the FEC,* allowed political parties to make independent expenditures; in other words, it said that party bosses could spend "independently" to support the candidates produced by the same party. Coming only months before an election, the case burst the floodgates: Both parties, particularly the Republicans, sent swarms of money to buttress the campaigns of congressional candidates.

The talking dog? No one knows the FEC's frustrations better than Lawrence Noble, the agency's general counsel. He defends the FEC like this: "Say you are walking down the street and you see a talking dog. Do you criticize its grammar, or are you amazed it talks

---

SOME WATCHDOG: "There's no fear of the FEC because by the time it gets there, elections are over and there's not much it can do. You may pay a fine, but you've won the race and it's over with."

Tony Coelho, former House member and major fund-raiser

at all?" Before harping on the FEC's inadequacies, Noble says, think about how remarkable it is that the agency exists—forcing disclosure and perhaps preventing even worse abuses.

By most accounts, the prospects for a true tightening of the campaign finance laws are slim. The likelihood they will be effectively enforced is slimmer still. The FEC has fought extinction since it was created. It has been stymied by Congress, starved of funds and saddled with weak commissioners. It faces courts that believe campaign regulations are a threat to free speech—and prefer to protect the latter. For now, it struggles on. But for a true measure of its impotence, consider this piece of black-letter law: No corporation or labor union can give anything of value to influence a federal election. Then consider the reality.

APPOINTEES: "The commissioners are appointed by congressional leaders. You get political payoffs, and so you get lower-quality people. Some of them don't believe in the law they're supposed to be enforcing."

Senate staffer who asked for anonymity

Scandal of the Past, Present and Future[4]

By Ellen Miller and Micah Sifry
IntellectualCapital.com, February 18, 1999

While the political establishment has been obsessing over whether President Clinton should be removed from office for breaking the law, there has been a telling bipartisan silence over an issue with far more importance for the future: The next president almost assuredly will get elected by breaking the law.

Not by committing perjury or obstruction of justice but by exploiting loopholes in the laws regulating campaign contributions to presidential candidates.

"More Loophole Than Law"

The Federal Election Campaign Act (FECA), enacted in 1971 and amended several times since, sets several conditions on fund-raising by presidential candidates. Contributions to their campaigns are limited to $1,000 per election and must come from individual citizens, not corporate or union treasuries. The only exception is for political action committees, which can give up to $5,000.

Pertinent information about each donor, including the name of his or her employer, is to be disclosed in a timely manner. Finally, FECA offers full public financing for the general election campaign to candidates who agree to raise no private money and gives matching funds to candidates who abide by spending limits for the primaries.

With each election, more and more of these rules have been disregarded, to the point where it is now safe to say we are back to the freewheeling days of the 1960s, when President Lyndon B. Johnson said the system is "more loophole than law." Pundits and pols who argue that the campaign-finance laws should be junked because everyone breaks them would never argue that the law against arson should be overturned because people keep setting fires.

The problem here is essentially a willful disregard for the intent and letter of the law, abetted by a politicized Federal Election Commission (appointed by Congress and the president) and a politicized

---

4. Article by Ellen Miller and Micah Sifry from *Intellectual Capital* February 18, 1999. Copyright © *Intellectual Capital.com*. Reprinted with permission.

Justice Department. These supposed enforcers of the law consistently have looked the other way as creative lawyers and determined candidates have pushed the envelope.

Among the first things to go were the individual state spending limits. Campaigns bypassed the cap for expenditures in, say, New Hampshire by renting cars and buying advertising in neighboring Massachusetts and charging those costs against their Massachusetts spending limit. But this was mere jaywalking compared with current practice.

Next to go was the decades-old prohibition on taking large contributions, as well as the solicitation of support from corporations. Enter "soft money."

Signs of a Replay of 1996?

The FEC has allowed the national and state parties to raise money outside the regulatory framework as long as it is used for generic "party-building" activities like get-out-the-vote drives. In

---

Until candidates formally file with the FEC, they can use personal political action committees as lucrative fund-raising vehicles.

---

practice, it is frequently used to benefit specific candidates. In 1996, the parties raised $263.5 million in soft money, three times as much as in the previous presidential election cycle.

The White House tapes of Clinton's infamous coffees for big donors capture the president boasting to one such gathering about how they used soft money to pay for what were essentially Clinton-Gore campaign ads. "We realized we could run these ads through the Democratic Party, which meant we could raise money in $20,000 and $50,000 and $100,000 wads," Clinton said.

The prohibition on soliciting donations while on government property, designed to prevent blatant shakedowns, is gone as well—unless some future attorney general decides to resurrect it. But Janet Reno decided that Vice President Al Gore had violated no law in making at least 56 calls to Democratic donors from his office because he was supposedly seeking money for generic party building, not his own campaign. The donors he called eventually coughed up at least $3.7 million.

Not to be outdone, the current crop of presidential candidates is showing as much creativity and ingenuity as their predecessors in subverting the rest of the law. It is no accident that they are all delaying the formal declaration of their candidacies while making multiple announcements about their intentions.

The reason is simple: Until candidates formally file with the FEC, they can use personal political action committees as lucrative fund-raising vehicles. These so-called "leadership PACs" can take donations of up to $5,000, fly the candidate all over the country, hire staff, pay for ads, schmooze donors—and none of this counts against the candidate's spending limit.

Several contenders, led by Republicans Lamar Alexander and former Vice President Dan Quayle, have gone one step further, setting up state-based versions of their federal PACs in order to take advantage of even more lenient conditions.

In Virginia, there are no limits on political contributions to PACs. A mere 81 donors gave Alexander a whopping $1.6 million by last fall, much of which he spent on clambakes in New Hampshire and TV ads in 10 states. A financial services company based in Portland, Ore., gave Quayle's Virginia PAC $250,000—50 times the allowable federal contribution.

Finally, at least one candidate, Steve Forbes, has established an "advocacy" organization that is actively soliciting contributions and spending money on political ads and disbursing favors on political allies—but completely outside the regulatory framework governing electoral activity.

Happy Birthday, Mr. President

But wait a minute, the real problem is not just the loopholes or the flawed regulatory structure; it is that money should not be the prime factor in determining who runs for president. Today, it is indeed the most formidable hurdle.

Since 1980, every candidate who has raised the most money by the beginning of the election year has won his party's nomination. Plenty of qualified leaders from across the political spectrum are deterred from running because of this plain fact. They do not want to be full-time fund-raisers.

Republican consultant Stan Huckaby estimates that a candidate will need $22 million by the end of 1999 to have a real chance of winning. That works out to more than $60,000 a day, or $41.86 an hour, that a presidential wannabe must raise—more than double what the average American earns in a year.

So the next time your child says he or she wants to grow up to be president, make sure his or her next birthday party is a fund-raiser.

II. Soft Money: PACs and Issue Advocacy

Editor's Introduction

Soft money remains one of the most controversial practices in campaign spending. Corporations and political action committees (more commonly known as PACs) use these unregulated contributions to circumvent federal limits on campaign fund-raising. The soft money loophole has resulted in huge increases in campaign spending that reform supporters would like to see reduced. Those in favor of reform point out that the voices of large donors, such as corporations or wealthy citizens, are often heard more easily than those of the average person. Corporations may also be rewarded with tax breaks and legislation that serves the interests of business over the interests of consumers.

Many people are familiar with the Watergate scandal that ended President Richard Nixon's administration, but few remember that campaign finance corruption also contributed to the president's undoing. The first article in this section, "Got Money?", demonstrates the connection between political contributions and policy in the Nixon White House, using the example of illegal contributions accepted from the dairy industry which resulted in changes that were beneficial to dairy farmers.

"Moving Money around Washington" discusses the role of political action committees, which can raise soft money in various ways, including gathering groups of individual contributions (a process known as "bundling") and "independent expenditures," which allow individuals or organizations to raise unlimited funds for a particular candidate. Next, "The New Money Game" looks at issue advertising, a form of political campaigning that is not regulated by campaign finance law. Although issue ads may not explicitly call for the election or defeat of a particular candidate, critics of such ads claim that the intent is clear.

The fourth article in this section, "Tobacco and Its Money Have Allies in New York," focuses on attempts by the tobacco industry to sway African American and Hispanic legislators through grants to local causes and campaign contributions. This report is followed by "Social *In*-Security," which examines efforts by Wall Street investors to use campaign contributions to influence Congress to privatize Social Security.

In "Bought and Paid For," *Salon* writer Mark Hertsgaard looks at the business connections of 2000 presidential candidates Al Gore and George W. Bush. The 2000 Republican and Democratic national conventions were sponsored by some of the biggest corporations in America in the hopes that their support would not be forgotten, a situation addressed by Mike Allen in "Corporate Cash Pours Into Conventions."

Finally, in "Campaign Overhaul Mired In Money and Loopholes," Karen Foerstel, Peter Wallsten, and Derek Willis contend that the two major parties and their candidates function as the most significant obstacles to reform through their willingness to take advantage of campaign finance loopholes.

Got Money?[1]

By Ron Schaumburg and Timothy Kelley
New York Times, March 27, 2000

On March 23, 1971, a group of dairy-industry leaders met with White House officials to ask for an increase in the federally supported price of milk. President Richard Nixon was gearing up for his reelection campaign and needed cash.

"Look here," Treasury Secretary John Connally told the President before the meeting. "If you have no objection, I'm going to tell them they've got to put so much money directly at your disposal."

The dairy industry had already pledged $1 million to Nixon's campaign, but the President wanted Connally to try to squeeze as much money from them as possible.

"He's used to shaking them down," Nixon later told an aide. "And maybe he can shake them for a little more."

It was that simple: The dairy industry wanted a favor, so in return, the President was asking, Got money?

Most people remember the Watergate scandal for the Nixon campaign's break-in at Democratic Party headquarters and the President's illegal efforts to cover it up. But the scandal that forced Nixon to resign in 1974 was also a campaign finance scandal, involving illegal contributions by the milk industry and others. And laws passed in response to it helped create the campaign finance system this year's Presidential candidates want to reform.

Money has been called "the mother's milk of politics," and it has long been employed in shady ways to buy political clout. In the late 1800s, companies routinely gave politicians money for governmental favors. This stirred calls for reform, and by the second decade of the 20th century, there were laws banning campaign contributions by companies and setting limits to what a campaign committee could spend for a candidate. But politicians and contributors always found ingenious ways around each new rule.

Charges of a White House deal with the dairy industry first came to light in 1972. But they were never explicitly confirmed until certain White House tapes were released in 1997, documenting one of the most blatant acts of campaign finance abuse in U.S. history.

---

1. From *New York Times Upfront*, March 27, 2000. Copyright © 2000 by Scholastic Inc. Reprinted by permission of Scholastic Inc.

On March 12, 1971, Secretary of Agriculture Clifford Hardin had announced that the price of milk would not be increased. On March 23, Nixon sat down with top dairy-industry leaders and said: ". . . you are a group that are politically very conscious. . . . And I must say, a lot of businessmen and others that I get around this table, they'll yammer and talk a lot, but they don't do anything about it. And you do, and I appreciate that. And I don't have to spell it out."

Later that day, they met with Connally. And some $322,500 from dairy groups soon poured into Nixon campaign committees. On March 25, Secretary Hardin changed his tune, announcing an "upward adjustment" in the milk price after all—a boon to dairy farmers.

The next January, consumer advocate Ralph Nader filed a lawsuit saying the increase was the result of "improper and unlawful influences" and would cost consumers millions. *The New York Times*

History suggests that keeping big money out of politics entirely is like keeping water from flowing downhill.

---

wrote: "Besides raising embarrassing questions about Republican campaign finance scruples in the short run, the allegations served to underline as nothing had done before the essentially undemocratic nature of much political fund-raising."

Soon, Americans learned of another proposed trade of favors for funds. The giant International Telephone and Telegraph Corporation (ITT) had offered to contribute $400,000 toward the expense of holding the 1972 Republican convention in San Diego, where Nixon wanted it. The gift wouldn't be an illegal contribution, ITT reasoned, because it would go through the city's tourist bureau. At the time, ITT wanted to merge with the Hartford Fire Insurance Company, and the Justice Department was blocking the deal on antitrust grounds.

On February 29, 1972, newspaper columnist Jack Anderson published what he said was a June 1971 memo from ITT lobbyist Dita Beard to her boss that linked ITT's contribution to its antitrust troubles: "I am convinced. . . that our noble commitment has gone a long way toward our negotiations on the mergers eventually coming out as [ITT's President] wants them. . . . [Attorney General John] Mitchell is definitely helping us, but it cannot be known . . . . Please destroy this, huh?"

Reporters asked Beard if the memo was genuine, and at first she said yes. Then she headed west on a vacation. Hospitalized in Denver for heart problems, she was visited by a man wearing pancake makeup and a crooked red wig. He was E. Howard Hunt, a former CIA spy working for Nixon's reelection committee. Shortly afterward, she changed her story and declared the memo a hoax. After the fuss, the convention was moved to Miami Beach. But the ITT merger went through.

Hunt also directed the burglars who made history at Democratic Party headquarters a few months later. Their bungled break-in was paid for with funds from a $200,000 campaign contribution from financier Robert Vesco. He, too, wanted a favor—an end to the investigation of his financial dealings by the Securities and Exchange Commission, the agency that monitors stock deals.

When the burglars threatened to reveal that they had been sent by the President's reelection committee, campaign cash came in handy once again. Nixon's lawyer, John Dean, went to the Oval Office on March 21, 1973, to warn him that it would take money to keep the burglars quiet:

Dean: We are being blackmailed. . . .

Nixon: How much money do you need?

Dean: I would say these people are going to cost a million dollars over the next two years.

Nixon: We could get that. . . .You could get it in cash. I know where it could be gotten. It is not easy, but it could be done.

These abuses spurred legislation in 1974 limiting individuals' campaign contributions to $1,000, and setting up new spending limits and a system of federal matching funds for Presidential candidates. But in 1976, the Supreme Court struck down the limits for campaigns that decline matching funds, opening the way to unlimited spending by rich candidates. It also allowed for so-called soft money, contributions that are unlimited because they go to parties instead of specific candidates.

This year, campaign finances have become an issue again, with some candidates proposing new reforms such as banning soft money. But history suggests that keeping big money out of politics entirely is like keeping water from flowing downhill.

Moving Money Around Washington[2]

A Brief Tour of "Bundling" and Other Beltway Bypasses

By Steven Hayward and Allison R. Hayward
Reason, October 1996

Campaign finance reform began not with Watergate but during the Progressive Era, when—not coincidentally—the first federal regulatory activities came into being. Theodore Roosevelt actually proposed public financing of elections in 1907, arguing that "if our political institutions were perfect, they would absolutely prevent the political domination of money in any part of our affairs." Though public financing was as much a nonstarter then as it is now, Congress did prohibit corporate campaign contributions. During World War II this ban on contributions was extended to labor unions.

But if corporate and labor union contributions are banned, how is it we so often read in the paper that some corporation has contributed thousands of dollars to a particular candidate, or that labor unions are planning to spend millions of dollars in this November's election? Corporations and labor unions are allowed to have their own political action committees, and although corporate funds may not be used for contributions, a corporation may pay the PAC's administrative expenses.

Corporations raise their money from a defined "restricted class" of employees, usually executives, administrators, shareholders, and their families. Corporations and their PACs are not allowed to communicate with their entire labor force. Labor unions, on the other hand, are technically "membership organizations," and as such can raise PAC funds directly through dues and "communicate" (which includes endorsing candidates) with all of their members. This is how labor unions are able to raise and spend millions without running afoul of the contribution limits or independent expenditure regulations. Strict contribution limits have led to a proliferation of alternative routes for money from organized interest groups. The biggest end run around the contribution limits is "soft money," which is a donation to the "non-federal" bank accounts of official political party committees, such as the Republican National Committee or Democratic National Committee.

"Soft money" is not tied to any individual candidate but is supposedly intended for "party-building" activities, such as voter registration drives and opinion polling. There are no limits on "soft money" contributions, which is why Dwayne Andreas of Archer-Daniels-Midland can give millions directly to both political parties and maintain the fiction that he isn't trying to buy ethanol subsidies because he doesn't contribute much directly to candidates. Charles Keating attempted to use this route to give more than $1 million indirectly to several senators in exchange for their calling off the bank regulators—but earmarked soft money (as well as the purchase of official action) are big no-nos in federal election law. Similarly, using another loophole, Andreas can allow Bob Dole and other politicians to fly on his private jet for the cost of a first class airline ticket, and it doesn't count as any kind of contribution or personal gift.

The second end run around the direct contribution limits is "bundling," in which a political organization rounds up a large number of individual contributions and forwards them to a favored candidate. This is the technique perfected by EMILY's List, which raises large sums for women Democratic candidates.

Finally, there is the "independent expenditure." PACs or individuals who feel especially strongly for or against a candidate can exercise their First Amendment right of free speech, launch a media campaign, and spend any sum of money they choose.

Independent campaign activities, however, must be "uncoordinated" with the candidate, although it is permissible (but risky) to "inform" the candidate of your plans. Organizations that engage in "indirect" political activity, such as GOPAC in the days when it was mostly a cassette tape distribution service and not a real PAC at all, are not subject to contribution limits or reporting requirements. Hence, a wealthy donor who faces a $5,000-per-election limit for contributions to a PAC can give unlimited amounts to organizations that do not formally support individual candidates. Such organizations, of course, provide a handy means for donors to give large sums to benefit the pet projects of their favorite politicians. The basic problem with campaign finance reform is that campaign contributions are like the proverbial toothpaste tube: Squeeze it here, and it will swell up somewhere else. The attempt to limit the influence of money in politics through regulation is futile so long as moneyed interests have so much at stake in what goes on in Washington. Interests will always find a way around the regulations to feed the politicians' insatiable demand for money. The only sure means of reducing the corrupting effect of money in politics is to reduce the size and scope of government.

The New Money Game[3]

BY ROMESH RATNESAR
TIME, NOVEMBER 2, 1998

Not so long ago, re-election looked like a breeze for New Jersey Representative Frank Pallone. A six-term Congressman in a district that tilts Democratic, he won his last two races handily with more than 60% of the vote. But this month an outfit called Americans for Job Security—in reality a front group led by large insurance companies furious with Pallone for heading the charge for managed-care reform—unveiled an anti-Pallone "issue ad:" the TV spot blasts Pallone's positions without explicitly advocating his defeat. Among other things, it accuses him of voting to raid the Social Security trust fund to pay for welfare. "Call Congressman Pallone," the announcer says, over a video of disreputable card sharks, "and tell him to . . . stop gambling with our futures." Pallone says the ad is false, but now he'll have to defend himself until Election Day. Americans for Job Security plans to spend $2 million to take him down.

Issue ads like these are flying under the radar of campaign-finance laws and into the living rooms of voters this election season. They came into vogue in 1996, when the AFL-CIO unleashed $20 million for ads targeting various members of Congress, and business groups retaliated. This year there's more money than ever going into making these ads, and more meanness being sunk into them.

Because the courts have ruled that issue ads are merely political opinions expressed by individuals or groups, rather than electioneering spots for a specific candidate, they are next to impossible to regulate. So interest groups and party affiliates—unlike the candidates themselves—don't have to disclose how much money they spend on advertising (or, in the case of independent groups, where the money comes from). This year more than 70 organizations have dumped at least $260 million into political issue ads, according to the Annenberg Public Policy Center. Many have appeared for the sole purpose of knocking off vulnerable candidates or just plain ideological enemies, much to the annoyance of campaign-finance crusaders. Grumbles reform advocate Fred Wertheimer: "It is one of the greatest fictions in American political history that these are [considered] issue ads as opposed to ads for the clear purpose of influencing federal elections."

---

3. Article by Romesh Ratnesar from *Time* November 2, 1998. Copyright © *Time*. Reprinted with permission.

While some prominent groups like the AFL-CIO are husbanding their resources this year for voter-mobilization drives, the political parties are getting in on the issue-ad bonanza. It's a doozy for Republicans. The National Republican Congressional Committee, which funds House races, figures to spend $28 million on issue ads in more than 30 states, a blitz dubbed Operation Breakout. That compares with $13 million in 1996. Democrats will spend $7 million, up $1 million from two years ago. The G.O.P. is expected to lay out $10 million on Senate races before the campaign is over. "The anticipation is excruciating—just thinking they're going to drop all this money in the last week, too late for us to respond," says a Democratic strategist.

Republican issue advertising has already played a major role in several tight contests. In South Carolina, incumbent Senator Ernest Hollings has spent twice as much as G.O.P. challenger Bob

---

Campaigns are increasingly fought on television, not on the streets, and the cost of air space limits what candidates can put out on their own.

Inglis since Labor Day, but Inglis has made up the gap through $725,000 in ads paid for by the state G.O.P. In Wisconsin's Senate race, squeaky-clean Democrat Russ Feingold refused to accept any party advertising on his behalf, but his challenger, Republican Mark Neumann, didn't make the same promise. Thanks to a three-month barrage of scathing anti-Feingold spots—none of which, of course, directly instruct viewers to vote against him—Neumann has closed a 27-point gap to zip.

There's good reason why the parties are busting through the issue-ad loophole. Campaigns are increasingly fought on television, not on the streets, and the cost of air space limits what candidates can put out on their own. And issue ads have advantages over spots that just say, "Vote for our guy." That kind of explicit shilling is subject to spending caps and can be paid for only with "hard" money—small contributions from individuals and political-action committees. An issue ad, though, can be funded in part with soft money, which parties can collect in any amount from virtually any

SPENDING ON ISSUE ADS IN MILLIONS (*projections)				
	Democrats		**Republicans**	
Committees	1996	1998*	1996	1998*
Congressional	$6	$7	$13	$28
Senatorial	$10	$10	$5.7	$10

source. The Republican National Committee and Ohio's Democratic Party are fighting in court for the right to pay for issue ads entirely with soft money.

Issue ads allow parties to do some of the candidates' dirty work. In Kentucky's barn-burning Senate race, the G.O.P. has poured close to $3 million into issue ads benefiting its candidate, Representative Jim Bunning. One ad engages in race baiting while hammering Bunning's opponent for voting for the North American Free Trade Agreement. "Tell Scotty Baesler, on foreign trade deals, start voting for Kentucky workers," the narrator says, "but if you live in Mexico you might want to tell him"—cut to a sloppily dressed, brown-skinned man—"Muchas gracias, Senor Baesler." The Republican pooh-bahs liked the ad so much that last week they rolled out another one, which hews to the same script but throws in a worker with Asian features who thanks Baesler in Chinese.

Some candidates have attested to a touch of discomfort with ads that convey misleading or offensive messages. But they are probably protesting too much. Issue ads serve to mercilessly savage an opponent's record and force sputtering denials. Yet if the spots come under fire for being too vicious, candidates can still say it wasn't their idea. What's not to like?

Plenty, for people concerned with the perniciousness of money in politics and the superficial, image-driven nature of campaigning. But there aren't too many of those folks in Congress these days. Campaign-reform efforts to regulate issue ads have foundered in Congress or have been blocked by the courts. And though labor and business groups spent most of their money this year on voter turn-out, they are already gearing up their advertising onslaughts for the 2000 presidential campaign. Now that the parties, too, have made issue advertising their campaign weapon of the future, it appears likely that the rest of us will be forced to see politics turned into a permanent, electronic spitting contest.

Tobacco and Its Money Have Minority Allies in New York[4]

By Clifford J. Levy
New York Times, January 4, 2000

State Senator Efrain Gonzalez Jr. of the Bronx decided to open a Washington office for a Hispanic legislators' association a few years ago, figuring that he would have little trouble raising the necessary $40,000. Following something of a tradition among black and Hispanic members of the New York Legislature, Mr. Gonzalez called a lobbyist for Philip Morris, and came away with the entire amount.

A colleague from the borough, Assemblywoman Gloria Davis, receives $5,000 annually from Philip Morris, the world's largest tobacco company, for a Thanksgiving meal for the poor in her predominantly black district. Seeking aid for a program to teach non-violence to young people, Ms. Davis said that she raised $22,000 from another cigarette giant, R. J. Reynolds.

Such corporate grants are not only a cornerstone in a decades-old campaign by the cigarette companies to foster good will in black and Hispanic neighborhoods, an important cigarette market. The grants have also helped the industry cement ties to black and Hispanic officials, who are often one of the few factions in the Democratic Party to oppose new restrictions on smoking.

While the industry is increasingly ostracized by many politicians in New York, some black and Hispanic state lawmakers depict it as a kindhearted corporate citizen, playing down the health consequences of smoking and asserting that they are not in a position to reject assistance from companies making legal products.

That alliance in New York, which has parallels in Washington and other state capitals, has until recently been a significant factor in the industry's enviable record in Albany. Even last month, when the tide suddenly turned against the tobacco companies in the Legislature for the first time since 1993, some black and Hispanic lawmakers came to their defense.

The lawmakers questioned a move by Gov. George E. Pataki and legislative leaders to pay for an expansion of health care for the uninsured in part by nearly doubling the cigarette tax, a measure

---

4. Article by Clifford J. Levy from *New York Times* January 4, 2000. Copyright © *New York Times*. Reprinted with permission.

that delighted antismoking groups. Ultimately, the lawmakers said they supported the bill because they did not want to hinder a new health-care program, but among Democrats, their views stood out.

"Another cigarette tax is a little out of hand," said Mr. Gonzalez, who until last month was president of the legislators' group, the National Hispanic Caucus of State Legislators. "It just looks sexy politically."

Antismoking groups say they are dismayed by the lawmakers' stances, contending that because blacks in particular smoke more and suffer higher rates of smoking-related illnesses than whites, the lawmakers should treat the industry more harshly. Such criticism has arisen before. But documents disclosed recently by the industry in smoking litigation cast the dispute in a new light, showing the extent of its generosity—and links to policymaking.

An internal Philip Morris document from 1988, for example, lists roughly 125 black groups that the company assisted across the nation: from the Bedford-Stuyvesant Real Estate Board (which received $200), to the Georgia Legislative Black Caucus ($6,000) to the National Association of Negro Business and Professional Women's Club ($12,000).

Next to some of the listings are the names of black politicians from New York and elsewhere who requested the grants. There is also a column titled "support on issues," which describes how some of the groups backed Philip Morris's effort to block smoking restrictions and cigarette taxes.

While Philip Morris did not disclose documents on its current giving, interviews indicate that it has not significantly diminished—indeed, the company is now seeking to soften its image by highlighting its philanthropy.

It donated $30,000 in 1998 to sponsor conferences for groups representing black and Hispanic New York lawmakers. The Bronx Democratic Committee, which is led by Assemblyman Roberto Ramirez, the most influential Hispanic politician in Albany, received $19,000 in the last three years from Philip Morris, and $10,000 more from R. J. Reynolds, according to campaign finance records.

In interviews, several black and Hispanic lawmakers scoffed at what they said was the heavy-handed approach of smoking opponents. They acknowledged that they were sympathetic to the industry because of its financial assistance, but dismissed suggestions of a quid pro quo.

And they said it was wrong to scrutinize their relationship to the tobacco industry while ignoring white lawmakers, especially Republicans, with similar ties.

"I don't think that I was sent to Albany to govern somebody's bedroom," Ms. Davis said. "We have enough laws on the books now."

The lawmakers said that in the past, when corporate America shunned black and Hispanic causes and had little interest in diversifying the work force, the tobacco companies were different.

"I can tell you that 25 years ago, when you could only get 10 people to show up for a caucus event, Philip Morris was always there," said Assemblyman Herman D. Farrell Jr., a Harlem Democrat who is the most powerful black lawmaker in Albany. He was referring to the Black, Puerto Rican and Hispanic Legislative Caucus in the State Legislature.

"Of course, today, it is looked upon as something nefarious," Mr. Farrell said. "Maybe we're addicted to that like you become addicted to cigarettes."

Peggy Roberts, a spokeswoman for Philip Morris, said the company was proud of its involvement with black and Hispanic lawmakers.

Tobacco

CENTER FOR RESPONSIVE POLITICS

Joe Camel and the Marlboro Man—A landmark settlement in 1997 between the tobacco industry and several state attorneys general promised the demise of these two smoking icons. However the nuts and bolts of that historic settlement, including plans to allow the Food and Drug Administration to regulate nicotine as a drug, were mostly scuttled when the industry spent millions of dollars lobbying Congress to block the deal.

The states later made another deal with the industry, on terms more favorable to cigarette makers, but tobacco's troubles are hardly over. Many of the issues raised in the first settlement package still are being debated in Washington today, while the Justice Department recently has announced plans to sue the tobacco industry to recoup federal costs linked to smoking-related illnesses.

At the same time, the tobacco industry continues to play a prominent presence in the funding of today's political campaigns. Here's a historical look at the industry's campaign contributions to federal parties and candidates, dating back more than two decades:

TOBACCO INDUSTRY CONTRIBUTIONS, 1979-2000

		Total	Dems	Repubs
1979-90	PACs	$6,102,903	$3,087,399	$3.011,804
1991-92	PACs	$2,298,950	$1,278,644	$1,020,106
	Soft Money	$2,807,739	$923,364	$1,884,375
	Individual Contributions	$624,439	$269,560	$348,960
	Total	$5,730,328	$2,471,568	$3,253,441
1993-94	PACs	$2,281,716	$1,149,067	$1,132,649
	Soft Money	$2,518,563	$356,150	$2,162,413
	Individual Contributions	$342,979	132,804	$209,875
	Total	$5,143,258	$1,638,021	$3,504,937
1995-96	PACs	$2,769,519	$667,098	$2,101,421
	Soft Money	$6,901,559	$1,064,680	$5,836,879
	Individual Contributions	$653,010	$159,000	$493,800
	Total	$10,324,088	$1,890,778	$8,431,560
1997-98	PACs	$2,340,002	$647,421	$1,691,581
	Soft Money	$5,470,542	$837,219	$4,633,323
	Individual Contributions	$616,269	$197,275	$418,994
	Total	$8,426,813	$1,681,915	$6,743,898
1999-00	PACs	$1,132,859	$351,790	$771,819
	Soft Money	$2,920,149	$237,500	$2,682,649
	Individual Contributions	$420,962	$116,500	$304,462
	Total	$4,473,970	$705,790	$3,758,930

Based on FEC data downloaded June 1, 2000. Totals include contributions to federal parties and candidates.

"Our history with diversity and minority employment goes back to the 50's," she said. "We are very anxious to build relationships with lots of different groups. These relationships are important to us, and if they help us get an understanding, or at least an audience with legislators from these communities, that is great."

Asked whether the company linked grants to official action, she said, "That's unfair. What we are trying to do is build relationships so that we can have a dialogue, and that is as far as it goes."

Representatives of R. J. Reynolds did not respond to several requests for comment.

Debates have long simmered over charitable giving by the tobacco companies, especially Philip Morris, which is among the biggest such benefactors in the nation and has carved a large role in financing the arts in New York City. Nonprofit groups have grappled with whether to refuse such money because it is generated in large part by profits from smoking. Many continue accepting it.

In places like Harlem, some groups have gone on campaigns against what they say is the tobacco companies' policy of flooding black and Hispanic neighborhoods with advertising and of aiming menthol-flavored brands like Newport, Kool and Salem at black smokers. Even so, many local politicians have remained on the sidelines.

A few have spoken out, including Assemblyman Albert Vann of Brooklyn. More common are the sentiments of black and Hispanic members of the Assembly Health Committee, which has been a battleground on the issue in recent years, particularly over a bill that would impose a state ban on smoking in restaurants.

In 1998, the bill's sponsors suffered a startling rebuff when four black and Hispanic Democrats on the Democratic-controlled committee—Ms. Davis, Mr. Ramirez, James Gary Pretlow of Westchester County and Darryl C. Towns of Brooklyn—voted with Republicans and killed the bill.

Saying that one of his primary concerns was economic development, Mr. Ramirez explained that he could not ignore the economic effects of more restrictions on his district. If fewer people smoke, then bodegas, which are often the backbone of Hispanic neighborhoods, will lose cigarette sales, he said.

White lawmakers, he said, "have the luxury and the flexibility of taking positions that are much more popular, because the consequences of their actions are never going to be felt in their districts."

Social *In*-Security[5]

COMMON CAUSE, FEBRUARY 1999

In the 106th Congress, the number one policy debate on Washington's agenda is Social Security reform. While a variety of reform proposals are on the table, one of the most talked about is privatization, or at least partial investment of the Social Security trust fund in the stock market.

Privatization, at a minimum, would mean billions of dollars in new investments for Wall Street. And, a new Common Cause analysis shows, those who have the most to gain have been giving millions of dollars in political contributions to Washington policy makers during the past decade.

With its wallet bulging from a decade of record-breaking stock market booms, the securities industry has given nearly $53 million to the national political parties and federal candidates since 1989, according to Common Cause.

Contributions from Wall Street interests included more than $37.4 million in soft money and more than $15.5 million in political action committee (PAC) contributions since 1989. The securities industry is the overall top soft money donor over the past decade, giving more than double what the tobacco industry gave during the same period, according to the analysis.

Securities interests have increased their soft money giving dramatically over the last several years. From January 1, 1997, to November 23, 1998, these interests invested $10.8 million of soft money into the national political parties, nearly double the $5.4 million the industry gave during 1993-1994, the last comparable period.

Morgan Stanley Dean Witter Discover & Co. is the top political contributor in the securities industry, giving $3 million in soft and PAC money since 1989. Goldman Sachs Group LP, Merrill Lynch & Co. Inc., and JP Morgan & Co. Inc. follow closely behind, according to Common Cause.

Slightly more than half of the industry's contributions went to Republicans who received $29.4 million compared to Democrats who received $23.5 million in PAC and soft money contributions since 1989. "The securities industry knows a good investment when it

---

5. Article from *www.commoncause.org* February 1999. Copyright © Common Cause. Reprinted with permission.

Top Soft Money Donors to National Political Parties by Industry January 1, 1989, through November 23, 1998

INDUSTRY	TOTAL
Securities	$37,434,557
Real Estate	$32,279,066
Entertainment and Media	$30,799,694
Insurance	$30,020,891
Labor Unions	$29,460,380
Oil and Gas	$29,336,098
Lawyers and Lobbyists	$24,063,874
Telecommunications	$19,134,767
Transportation	$18,026,928
Pharmaceuticals	$17,991,586
Tobacco	$17,789,601

sees one. While Americans wonder which Social Security proposal will win in Congress this session, Wall Street's tycoons are brokering deals with huge political contributions," Common Cause President Ann McBride said. "This year, Congress must work to ensure that today's seniors—and future seniors—are not thrust into poverty simply because Washington catered, once again, to special interests."

The Social Security Administration predicts that under current economic projections and tax rates, as baby boomers begin to retire, the Social Security program will owe more money in benefits than it collects from payroll taxes and will eventually go broke. Three possible fixes have been proposed—raising taxes, reducing benefits, or privatizing a portion of the program by investing it in the stock market. Thanks to generous campaign contributions, persistent lobbying by Wall Street interests and a booming stock market, privatization is gaining in popularity as an avenue of reform in Washington, according to Common Cause. The most radical privatization proposals would reduce the Social Security tax, while setting up personal investment accounts to let individuals invest the difference where they wish. President Clinton, in his State of the Union address, advocated taking a part of the budget surplus and investing it in the stock market, a plan many Republicans have criticized for not going far enough.

Bought and Paid For[6]

By Mark Hertsgaard
Salon, January 21, 2000

Vice President Al Gore delivered a scathing speech back on Oct. 7, 1997, at Georgetown University in Washington chiding those who "ignore the scientific warnings [about global warming] and continue stubbornly on our current course." How will our children and grand-children ever forgive us, Gore asked, if we do not act in the face of overwhelming evidence that burning more oil and coal is changing the earth's climate?

On that very same day, thanks to recommendations Gore made as part of his crusade to "reinvent government," the Department of Energy announced that Occidental Petroleum was buying the Elk Hills reserve in California, 47,000 acres of oil-rich, publicly owned land that had been off-limits to commercial development since 1912. President Nixon had tried to open up Elk Hills to private interests in 1973, after the first oil shock. President Reagan tried three separate times to do the same. Each time, Congress blocked the sale. But Al Gore, with President Clinton's help, succeeded.

The purchase of Elk Hills tripled Occidental Petroleum's domestic oil reserves overnight. It also enriched Occidental's stockholders, including Gore's father, Al Gore Sr. The elder Gore owned more than $500,000 worth of Occidental stock at the time of the Elk Hills purchase in 1997. When he died the following year, his son became the executor of his estate and, according to the vice president's federal income disclosure forms, the estate continued, as of May 1999, to hold the Occidental stock.

The close relationship Gore and his father have enjoyed with Occidental Petroleum is detailed in "The Buying of the President 2000," a new book by Charles Lewis and the Center for Public Integrity. Lewis is the founder and executive director of the center, a nonpartisan watchdog group of journalists in Washington whose scoops include the Lincoln Bedroom fund-raising scandal. A former investigative reporter with "60 Minutes" and ABC News, Lewis founded the Center for Public Integrity in 1990. In two previous books, "The Buying of the President" (1996) and "The Buying of the Congress," and nearly 40 reports, the center's journalists have relentlessly illuminated one of the most important political stories in the United

---

6. Article by Mark Hertsgaard from *Salon* January 21, 2000. Copyright © *Salon*. Reprinted with permission.

States today: what politicians appear to do in return for their biggest funders. For any American who doesn't want to be a chump this election year, "The Buying of the President 2000" is an essential read. It also has the promise of making life miserable for every leading presidential candidate—if the nation's political journalists take the trouble to read the book.

"The Buying of the President 2000" reports that Occidental gave $50,000 after one of Gore's fund-raising calls from his White House office. "Indeed," according to the book, "since Gore became part of the Democratic ticket in the summer of 1992, Occidental has given more than $470,000 in soft money to various Democratic committees and causes." And Gore himself has received $35,550 in Occidental campaign contributions during that same period, the center estimates.

And there's much, much more: Lewis' fascinating dissection of the more than 50-year relationship between Gore's family and Occidental Petroleum begins when the elder Gore was serving in the House of Representatives. Occidental was then run by Armand Hammer, once described as "the godfather of American corporate corruption" and a master of double-dealing who laundered funds and placed spies in the United States for Moscow to protect his vast oil and gas holdings in the Soviet Union. Hammer buddied up to Gore Sr. by putting him on the payroll of his New Jersey cattle ranch in the 1940s. FBI Director J. Edgar Hoover wanted to prosecute Hammer, but backed off for fear of Hammer's friends in Congress, including Gore, who ascended to the Senate in 1952. Before long, charges "The Buying of the President 2000," the advantages of being friends with Hammer were inevitably passed on to Gore Jr.

In the 1960s, when zinc ore was discovered near the Gore farm in Tennessee, Hammer bought the land, sold it to Gore Sr. and then paid him $20,000 per year for the mineral rights. Gore Sr. later sold the land to his son, who has received the $20,000 every year since (though the mineral rights were transferred in 1985 to Union Zinc). When Gore Sr. left the Senate in 1970, "Hammer gave him a $500,000-a-year job as the chairman of Island Coal Creek Company, an Occidental subsidiary, and a seat on Occidental's board of directors," according to the book. Meanwhile, Al Jr. and his wife, Tipper, hosted Hammer at Ronald Reagan's 1984 inauguration and again at President Bush's in 1988. "In return," according to the book, "Hammer and members of his family bent over backwards to get money into Gore's campaigns," and the largesse continued after Hammer died, in 1990, and Gore became Clinton's vice president.

Public Citizen
1997/1998 Campaign Finance Facts and Figures
Total Funds

- In the 1998 election cycle, federal candidates and national parties raised $1.45 billion, 19% more than the $1.22 billion raised for the comparable 1994 mid-term election.

Soft Money

- Total Soft Money contributions (unlimited contributions from corporations, labor unions, and individuals) to the two major parties for the 1998 congressional election cycle: $224.4 million, more than twice the $101.7 million raised for the 1994 mid-term election.
- Democratic party committees raised $92.8 million in soft money (41% of the total), while Republican party committees raised $131.6 million (59% of the total).
- Top Economic Sectors Donating Soft Money: Business: $121.2 million; Labor $10.2 million. Republicans: Securities & Investments $9.1 million; Insurance $8.6 million; Oil & Gas $6 million. Democrats: Labor $10 million; Lawyers & Lobbyists $6.5 million; Securities & Investments $6.3 million.
- Top Soft Money Donors: Phillip Morris $2.4 million; Communications Workers of America $1.5 million; American Federation of State/Cnty/Munic Employees $1.3 million; American Financial Group $1.3 million; American Financial Group $1.3 million, Amway $1.3 million; RJReynolds $1.1 million.

Hard Money

- Senate and House candidates raised $781.3 million in hard money (contributions limited by federal law), 6% more than the $740.5 million raised in 1994.
- Democratic candidates raised $367.5 million (47% of all hard money), Republican candidates raised $408.8 million (52%), and third party candidates raised $5 million (1%).
- Senate: average winning candidate spent $5.2 million; average losing candidate spent $2.8 million. 90% of incumbents were re-elected. House: average winning candidate spent $650,000; average losing candidate spent $211,000. 98% of incumbents were re-elected.
- Total PAC contributions to House and Senate candidates: $219.9 million, a 16% increase from the $189.6 million contributed in 1994. Democrats: $103 million, Republicans: $116.4 million (78% to incumbents, 10% to challengers, and 12% to open seat candidates).
- Democratic party committees raised $160 million in hard money, a 15% increase from the $139.1 million raised in the 1994 election. Republican party committees raised $285 million, a 16% increase from the $245.6 million raised in 1994.

Occidental, meanwhile, appears to be a particularly toxic friend for Gore to have. The company, in the form of its subsidiary, Hooker Chemical, was responsible for one of the great environmental tragedies of modern American history, the contamination of Love Canal, N.Y. Of course, Gore claimed a few weeks ago on the campaign trail that it was he who "discovered" the Love Canal tragedy and publicized it through Senate hearings, which makes his familial ties to the company especially embarrassing.

Laura Quinn, a Gore spokeswoman, said she saw no contradiction between Gore's environmental reputation and his opening of Elk Hills to commercial development. She disputed that Gore's actions were in any way a form of favoritism to Occidental. "The vice president doesn't have the ability to rule firms in or out of a federal bidding process," said Quinn. "A number of other firms bid on Elk Hills, and Occidental Petroleum was chosen because it offered twice as much as anyone else did."

It's probably cold comfort to Gore, but "The Buying of the President 2000" also reports incriminating information about Texas Gov. George W. Bush, in particular his long and friendly relationship with the Harvard Management Company, the private investment firm whose only client is the multibillion-dollar endowment of Harvard University.

Of course, Harvard has been the intellectual den of iniquity the Republican faithful love to hate ever since Richard Nixon's dark mutterings about the ultra-liberal Harvard professors in John F. Kennedy's White House. But Nixon could never voice such charges without sounding slightly creepy. Bush manages to make a joke of them, like when a reporter, during a recent debate, invoked a Harvard professor's opinion while pressing Bush on a question. "Consider the source," Bush cracked, eyes twinkling. Instantly, the crowd burst into laughter.

Give him credit for nerve. According to "The Buying of the President 2000," a close relationship between Bush and Harvard Management began in 1986, when the company helped bail out one of his failing oil companies, Harken Oil and Gas, by investing at least $20 million in it. Then, in 1990, when Bush suddenly unloaded two-thirds of his shares in Harken—netting a profit of nearly $850,000—two months before the company's debt restructuring sent its stock price plummeting, Harvard Management appears to have been the silent partner that took the unwanted shares off his hands. The move triggered an insider-trading investigation by the Securities and Exchange Commission.

And in 1995, when he was governor of Texas, Harvard Management had secured a real-estate deal from the pension fund of Texas's 800,000 public school teachers—buying a Dallas hotel, without a public bid, for $27 million less than the pension fund had spent on building improvements alone. And, for that matter, Bush did make it into Harvard Business School despite having a mere C average in college.

"These allegations are totally ridiculous and simply not true," said Scott McClellan, spokesman for the Bush campaign. Regarding Harvard's investments in Harken Oil and Gas, McClellan said, "The SEC said there was nothing there." As for the hotel purchase from the teachers fund, he said, "Apparently there's a lack of understanding of how state government works, because in 1995 the board [of the fund] was controlled by former [Democratic] Gov. Anne Richards' appointees." Harvard Management offered only a "no comment."

The book also chronicles how Wall Street investment firms have long been Bill Bradley's foremost financial patrons, while John McCain has been the beneficiary of major donations from the gambling industry. It reports on dozens of other similarly incriminating "coincidences" in its 342 densely argued pages, and none of the leading candidates, nor their sponsors at the Democratic and Republican national committees, get off easy.

Why hasn't this book sparked a firestorm of coverage and determined inquiry from the rest of the news media? Some activists angry at Occidental for drilling a pipeline through the Colombian rain forest have begun to heckle Gore, chanting, "What about Occidental? What about Occidental?" But generally, there hasn't been much of a ripple caused by the book's publication. Every political journalist in the country has been alerted to the book's publication. And certainly Lewis and the center have a proven record of fairness and reliability. "We're obviously disappointed we haven't gotten more press for this book," said Lewis.

The most optimistic explanation for the media's silence is that reporters just haven't gotten around to reading "The Buying of the President 2000" yet, or perhaps they're taking the time to independently investigate and verify the book's charges before sharing them with the public. Of course, citizens are free to go buy the book themselves. But first they have to hear about it.

Corporate Cash Pours Into Conventions[7]

BY MIKE ALLEN
WASHINGTON POST, JULY 28, 2000

Twenty-five years after Congress approved federal funding for national political conventions in an effort to create pure civic exercises, the cost of this year's nominating extravaganzas has soared past $100 million, reducing the official money to little more than a down payment on a high-tech playground for donors and lobbyists. Each of the major parties received $13.5 million from the Treasury Department to stage this summer's conventions. Republicans kick off on Monday in Philadelphia, and Democrats follow two weeks later in Los Angeles.

Because of the federal money, the parties may not take cash subsidies from corporations, although they do accept plane and train tickets, the use of cars and computers, and Web services.

But the federal funding, which was created by a law signed by President Gerald R. Ford as one of the reforms arising from Watergate, accounts for just under one-fourth of this year's tab. The rest was raised by "host committees" in Philadelphia and Los Angeles. The committees can accept unlimited, tax-deductible gifts, then use them to create sprawling convention complexes for the parties.

"Without private money, the conventions as we know them today would not exist," said Eli Broad, a businessman who is co-chairman of the host committee for the Democrats, L.A. Convention 2000, and has personally contributed $1.1 million to the effort.

The host committee for the Republicans, Philadelphia 2000, is spending $12 million just to outfit the convention hall, Comcast-Spectacor's First Union Center, including building the stage and media pavilions, remodeling the skyboxes and upgrading utilities.

Those footing the bill include 10 "platinum benefactors" who donated $1 million in cash or services. L.A. Convention 2000 has 11 "primary partners" who donated $1 million or more in cash or services.

It was just such largess that Congress was trying to avoid in late 1974 when it passed a law that provided for public financing for conventions (starting in 1976 at $5.5 million each) as part of the sweeping campaign finance overhaul that provided matching

---

7. Article by Mike Allen from the *Washington Post* July 28, 2000. Copyright © *Washington Post.* Reprinted with permission.

funds for primaries and public funding for general election campaigns, paid for by the checkoff on tax returns. In return, contributions and spending were limited.

The change was seen as so revolutionary that Rep. Wayne L. Hays, an Ohio Democrat, asserted that if such controls had been in place, "Watergate would never have happened."

Convention financing came into the spotlight in 1972 with the disclosure by columnist Jack Anderson and his associate Brit Hume, now the Fox News star, of a memo by lobbyist Dita Beard suggesting that International Telephone and Telegraph Corp. had agreed to raise $400,000 for that year's Republican convention—at the time, a huge share of the cost—as an incentive for the Justice Department to settle its antitrust case against ITT.

After the scandals involving President Richard M. Nixon, the Democratic and Republican parties became so concerned about the perception that large checks were corrupting them that they held a joint meeting in 1974 to consider new ways to finance conventions. They discussed a national telethon and lotteries by state parties.

At that time, much of the money for conventions was raised by selling ads in the programs. In 1972, each party charged $10,000 a page. Republicans raised $1.7 million and Democrats raised $980,000.

Now, with the host committee system, one company can give that much: For the 1996 Republican convention in San Diego, organizers credited AT&T with donating $2 million in cash and services. AT&T is back this year on both $1 million lists, and is providing calling cards for the delegates' goodie bags. (Democrats can also look forward to pillows from Hilton, while Republicans will get elephant-shaped macaroni from Kraft and Convention Barbie by Mattel.)

Democratic National Committee officials said the party supports taxpayer financing of conventions as a critical part of the post-Watergate reforms. But Jim Nicholson, chairman of the Republican National Committee, said he would support the repeal of taxpayer funding. "I think the political parties should put on the conventions without it," he said.

Nevertheless, the RNC has a promotional deal with Amtrak, including a link to the railroad's Web site from the party's convention Web site (*www.gopconvention.com*). Also, a headline in the June issue of Attache, the in-flight magazine of US Airways, blares: "US Airways Named Official Airline for Republican National Convention."

The Democratic Party makes similar deals. General Motors is the "transportation partner" of the Democratic National Convention, United is the official airline and *Event411.com* is "the official online event-planning provider."

David F. Girard-diCarlo, co-chairman of Philadelphia 2000 and managing partner of a major Philadelphia law firm, said he sees nothing sinister in the gifts. "I'm sure there are people who give because they want access and, to be candid, what's wrong with that?" said Girard-diCarlo, who is Pennsylvania chairman of George W. Bush's presidential campaign. "All of life is built on relationships."

The $1 million donor list in both cities includes Microsoft Corp., one of the many major contributors facing high-stakes issues involving the federal government. Microsoft is giving $100,000 in cash and $900,000 in software and services to each convention. "We're quite proud to support the political process, and I think people know that and appreciate that support," said Rick Miller, a Microsoft spokesman. "I don't think we're looking for any benefit beyond that."

United Parcel Service is giving about $1 million in cash and services to each convention, including loaning logistics executives to the organizers for the past six months. Tad Segal, the company's Washington director of public relations, said the draw is "brand exposure and business development."

The U.S. government accounts for 70 percent of the sales of Lockheed Martin Corp., the aerospace and defense giant, which is giving $100,000 to each convention. Hugh Burns, a corporate spokesman, said the donation is "part of good government—we support the democratic process."

General Motors, which is on both million-dollar lists, has loaned a fleet of cars to each convention as part of a tradition that goes back to the 1950s. This year, each party will get the use of about 400 vehicles. For the GOP, that includes 100 Buick LeSabres, 20 minivans and six Chevy Suburbans, but no Cadillacs. The Democratic manifest includes 48 Cadillac Sevilles and 10 Cadillac DeVilles. "It's a tremendous opportunity to expose these products to a diverse and influential group," said Bill Noack, GM's director of public policy communications.

The host committees do not have to disclose their donors until 60 days after the convention. But the Los Angeles committee said it has posted all of its major donors on its Web site (*www.lahost2000.org*), and the Philadelphia committee said it listed most of them in its Official Delegate & Media Guide. A Philadelphia committee official said no donor insisted on secrecy, although some ignored faxed and phoned requests for permission to include them on the list, and so were omitted.

TOP CONVENTION DONORS	
Givers of $1 million or more to the national conventions	
Republican	**Democratic**
AT&T	AIG
Ballard Spahr Andrews & Ingersoll	AT&T
Bell Atlantic	BP Amoco
City of Philadelphia	General Motors
Comcast	Maguire Partners
Commonwealth of Pennsylvania	Microsoft
Delaware River Port Authority	Motorola
General Motors	SBC
PECO Energy	Staples Center
	SunAmerica
	United Parcel Service

SOURCES: Convention host committees

L.A. Convention 2000 incorporated the logos of its million-dollar sponsors on the 2,500 street pole banners it began hanging in April.

Sponsors get little else that is tangible, according to organizers, who contend that almost all of the donations are made out of civic pride. (Federal regulations require corporate donors to have a presence in the metropolitan area where the convention is held, but the Federal Election Commission has interpreted that loosely.)

A GOP source says someone who donates $100,000 to the host committee gets one credential, whereas two credentials could likely be obtained with a much smaller donation to a national Republican campaign committee.

"If you are a giver who is looking to influence federal policy, then I can't imagine a more inefficient way to do it than to give it to a host committee for a convention," said David L. Cohen, a Philadelphia 2000 co-chair who is chairman of a large Philadelphia law firm.

Whatever the reasons for giving, financial reports for the 1996 convention reflect the corporations' thoroughness in underwriting the fun that begins after the speeches end. At the Democratic convention in Chicago, for instance, Miller Brewing Co. chipped in $15,000 in beer and $600 in mugs, while Anheuser-Busch Cos. donated $5,500 in beer and $200,000 in cash.

The Marshall Field's department store sprang for $78,500 in cash—and $45 in mints.

Campaign Overhaul Mired in Money and Loopholes[8]

BY KAREN FOERSTEL AND PETER WALLSTEN WITH DEREK WILLIS
CONGRESSIONAL QUARTERLY WEEKLY, MAY 13, 2000

With the White House at stake and Congress in play, campaign cash is flowing this year like a bulging stream in a flash flood. Where is the record level of money coming from? Who gets it?

These are the questions on the minds of strategists and analysts, but more than ever before in modern American history, the answers are not clear. Politicians and their benefactors are forever finding holes in an already loophole-laden campaign finance system that, at one time, aimed to curb the impact of big money and assure public disclosure of those trying to influence elections.

In 2000, the leaders of both major parties and candidates across the nation are seizing upon new ways to avoid money limits and disclosure requirements. They have established nonprofit advocacy groups that raise and spend money in the shadows. They have shifted millions of dollars between state and national party organizations and used so-called soft money to avoid contribution limits. There is no evidence that anyone is breaking the law. As the Senate prepares to discuss a campaign finance overhaul at a hearing May 17, advocates of changing the system say the real scandal is that the law lets politicians avoid disclosure.

"In the world we live in today, practically speaking, there are no limits on what you can give to a campaign," said Larry Makinson, executive director of the Center for Responsive Politics, a Washington watchdog group that tracks political fund-raising. "The Federal Election Commission is more useless than ever—and so are we. We're looking at a shrinking pie of reportable money, and it's frightening."

The Federal Election Commission (FEC) estimates that even without unreported money, a record-breaking $3 billion will be spent on this year's presidential and congressional races. According to the FEC, every election cycle since 1992 had set a federal spending record. Overall campaign finance activity has nearly doubled in the past 12 years.

---

8. Article by Karen Foerstel and Peter Wallsten with Derek Willis from *Congressional Quarterly Weekly* May 13, 2000. Copyright © *Congressional Quarterly Weekly*. Reprinted with permission.

And little of that money comes from average voters, say political watchdog groups. According to the Center for Public Integrity, a nonprofit organization that tracks political giving, less than 5 percent of Americans contribute to political campaigns, and less than one-quarter of 1 percent give $200 or more. "All the other money is coming from businesses and organizations with ulterior motives," said Peter Eisner, the center's managing director.

Eisner's group and other advocates of change say large donations from a relatively few wealthy individuals and special-interest groups have a significant influence on public policy, from sugar subsidies to tomato tariffs to Internet taxes to rules for mobile homes.

Others say the problem is time, not influence-peddling. Former Rep. Al Swift, D-Wash. (1979-95), who led a campaign fund-raising overhaul effort in the 1980s, said he believes money has become the deciding factor in winning elections—and not necessarily because it buys votes. "I don't think you can buy public policy," Swift said. "I'm more concerned about the time spent raising it."

The political landscape in 2000 presents a dilemma for advocates of a campaign finance overhaul.

Rep. Charles W. Stenholm, D-Texas, said the fund-raising strategies that worked when he first won his seat in 1978 do not suffice any more. "Going down and having to spend hour after hour after hour on personal calls, I hate doing that," said Stenholm, who raised more than $1.5 million in the 1998 cycle in the face of a stiff challenge. "I did it last time because I had to." The fund-raising can be so intense, Stenholm said, that colleagues often duck out of the Capitol during key meetings and can be found at party campaign headquarters "dialing for dollars."

Swift and the watchdog groups agree that even more disturbing than the huge amounts of money flowing through campaign committees are the millions of dollars spent by outside groups that never gets reported to the FEC.

It is all legal under the "527" tax code provision. Under this newly discovered loophole in tax and campaign law, millions of dollars are being raised by special groups that do not have to disclose their contributors. They are difficult to track, let alone outlaw, and those who want to eliminate the groups face constitutional obstacles. Group organizers say they are expressing their First Amendment right to free speech. Even foreign countries can give money to affect the outcome of American elections.

"All the fund-raising problems that happened in 1996 with foreign money can now be done legally and anonymously," Markinson said. The groups "are the most dangerous loophole that's ever existed in American politics."

Limited Legislation

The political landscape in 2000 presents a dilemma for advocates of a campaign finance overhaul. While the maverick presidential campaign of Sen. John McCain, R-Ariz., placed the issue at center stage, both parties' record-breaking fund-raising success gives incumbents little incentives to support change.

Several bills—including one (HR 4168) by Rep. Lloyd Doggett, D-Texas, and one (HR 3688) by Rep. Dennis Moore, D-Kan.—have been introduced in the 106th Congress to close the ""527" loophole, a name that comes from the tax code provision that exempts the contributions raised by certain political organizations from taxation. However, none of those bills are expected to get so much as a hearing. Meanwhile, Sen. Joseph I. Lieberman, D-Conn., often mentioned as a possible vice presidential contender, plans to introduce two proposals May 17 to tackle "527," with McCain as a cosponsor. One would require the groups to comply with federal election disclosure laws, and the other would require "527s" to register with the IRS and disclose donor information.

The only campaign finance bill poised to get a hearing this year is a measure (S 1816) by Sen. Chuck Hagel, R-Neb., that is scheduled to be discussed by the Rules and Administration Committee on May 17 and marked up June 14. But while Hagel's bill would limit soft money contributions to parties and committees from corporations and labor unions, it would not address the phenomenon of unreported political money. It also is silent on the parties' common practice of shifting money between national and state organizations, a strategy that would easily circumvent Hagel's soft money limits.

Even bill supporters say the measure would do little to stem the flood of campaign money. "If I started loading on to this bill every perceived problem to cure every perceived ill, I think the reality is it would go nowhere," Hagel said in an interview May 2. McCain, whose presidential bid won only four Senate endorsements, including Hagel's, offered a blunt commentary on Hagel's bill in a May 2 interview: "It's a joke."

The House passed legislation (HR 417) in 1999 that would ban soft money in federal elections and crack down on "issue advocacy," unregulated political spending that does not directly urge the election or defeat of a candidate. McCain and Russell D. Feingold, D-Wis., offered a similar measure (S 1593) in the Senate, but a filibuster engineered by Rules and Administration Committee Chairman Mitch McConnell, R-Ky., and Majority Leader Trent Lott, R-Miss., prevented passage.

Most agree the chances of passing significant legislation this year are slim. "The political reality is that this is a presidential election year," Hagel said. "Need we say more?"

Political Impact

Even if Congress does not act on campaign finance, McCain's ability to turn the issue into the centerpiece of his presidential campaign put it center stage for the political season. McCain may have lost the GOP nomination to Texas Gov. George W. Bush, but he forced other candidates to take a stand. Now they are finding that the issue can be a useful tool.

Vice President Al Gore, the presumptive Democratic presidential nominee, has promised to make McCain's bill his first domestic policy initiative. It could prove politically astute for a candidate dogged by criticism for his 1996 fund-raising tactics, including a gathering at a Buddhist temple in California.

Bush unveiled an overhaul plan earlier this year as he scurried to halt McCain's threat in the GOP primaries. The Bush plan would ban corporate and union soft money, but would allow unlimited contributions by individuals, a change that McCain said in the campaign would do little to curb big money. Bush has not made campaign finance a centerpiece of his campaign, though the issue could enhance his outsider status. Despite their differences, McCain endorsed Bush on May 9 after a brief meeting in Pittsburgh during which they discussed several issues, including campaign finance—but McCain conceded that they came to no agreement on the issue.

McConnell is a longtime opponent of campaign finance changes. But he said in an interview that Hagel's bill "seems to be a step or an approach toward campaign finance that might receive bipartisan approval." McConnell is chairman of the National Republican Senatorial Committee (NRSC), which raised $40.4 million between Jan. 1, 1999, and March 31, 2000. He opposes contribution limits because he says they violate First Amendment free speech rights. McConnell said he has not decided whether to support Hagel's plan.

Democrats have jumped on the issue in the battle for control of the House, filing a civil racketeering lawsuit against Majority Whip Tom DeLay, R-Texas, for his fund-raising tactics. The Democratic Congressional Campaign Committee (DCCC filed the suit May 3, accusing DeLay of extorting campaign funds from lobbyists by exchanging policy for money and intimidating donors who tend to favor Democrats.

DeLay denied that he had broken the law, but did not disagree with the notion that he was using the nonprofit groups for campaign purposes. Rep. Patrick J. Kennedy, D-R. I., chairman of the DCCC, said that if the courts do not stop DeLay and the Republicans, they will stockpile money in secret places, and Democrats will be at a huge disadvantage in November. "We could be up against something that we don't know the full extent of, nor do the American people know the full extent of this," Kennedy told reporters May 3.

But the contradiction inherent in calling for an overhaul of a system that allows everyone to raise unprecedented sums, according to scholars, raises questions about everybody's sincerity.

"Frankly, McConnell is pursuing [Hagel's bill] as a way of deflecting political pressure," said Thomas E. Mann, who studies campaign finance issues at the Brookings Institution, a Washington think tank. "And the Democrats, they're doing so well in the soft money raising business now, especially through their campaign committees, that they're not so anxious to eliminate it."

The contradiction inherent in calling for an overhaul of a system that allows everyone to raise unprecedented sums . . . raises questions about everybody's

McConnell, as his party's top Senate campaign strategist, also must walk a tightrope on the campaign finance issue, with several GOP incumbents facing tough challenges in November.

"You've got a lot of nervous Republicans, particularly a lot of nervous Republicans up" for re-election, said Norman J. Ornstein, resident scholar at the American Enterprise Institute, a Washington think tank. Opposing campaign finance changes "makes you look foolish if you have a Republican Party that uses as its core strategy against Al Gore his campaign finance violations. If you're saying what Al Gore did is outrageous and wrong but the system is dandy, that's not a tenable position."

Sen. Spencer Abraham, R-Mich., for example, is facing an intense challenge from Democratic Rep. Debbie Stabenow in a state whose GOP primary voters backed McCain over Bush. Abraham, who did not support the McCain-Feingold bill, has signed on as a cosponsor of the Hagel bill. "He does talk about it" on the campaign trail, said spokesman Joe Davis. "He thinks campaign finance reform is on the voters' minds." Abraham had raised $6.5 million for his campaign as of March 31. Stabenow had raised $3.4 million.

Sen. John Ashcroft, R-Mo., also is in a tenuous re-election position. Asked whether he had decided to ask McConnell or Lott to pass a campaign finance bill, Ashcroft said, "Not yet." But Ashcroft's opponents at home hope the issue will haunt him on the campaign trail in November.

That is when advocates for public campaign financing hope to put an initiative on the Missouri ballot, similar to one that has passed in Maine and is being debated in Oregon, which would allow tax-payer-financed campaigns for state offices.

Ashcroft "will be forced to take a position on it," said Harriett Woods, a former Democratic lieutenant governor of Missouri and unsuccessful Senate candidate. She is on the steering committee for the state ballot initiative and a member of the national advisory board of Public Campaign, a nonprofit organization that promotes limiting the power of special interests in elections through state-level initiatives.

Woods said that as more states approve campaign changes such as public financing, Congress might take notice. "Every time a state passes it, the congressional delegation is on the hot seat," she said.

The PAC controversy began to subside in the 1990s, as both parties mastered PAC fund-raising and a new form of campaign cash emerged: soft money.

Changing Loopholes

The DCCC lawsuit may be the first effort of the new century to politicize campaign fund-raising, but lawmakers have made political hay of the issue since the turn of the last century.

During his annual message to Congress in 1905, President Theodore Roosevelt called for a ban on corporate donations to political committees. Roosevelt's call for reform came after congressional hearings revealed that several corporations had secretly financed Roosevelt's 1904 campaign.

Efforts to overhaul the campaign system have generally surfaced in the wake of political scandal—and when one party has benefited from a campaign finance loophole more than the other.

During the 1970s and '80s, contributions from political action committees (PACs) exploded, with Democrats as the main beneficiaries. In the 1978 elections, PACs contributed $35 million to federal candidates. That rose to $60 million in 1980 and to $159 million by 1990.

During the 1988 congressional elections, House Democrats took in 66 percent of all PAC contributions. Republicans received 34 percent. The lopsided giving to Democrats continued until 1996, when PAC donations split evenly between both parties in the House.

Political watchdog groups charged that the hefty PAC donations gave big corporations special access to elected officials, who were beholden to their financial backers.

Congress attempted to curb PACs in 1989 after former Speaker Jim Wright, D-Texas (1955-89), came under attack for ethical violations and questionable financial dealings. The controversy put pressure on House Democrats to act on campaign finance legislation. Wright appointed a bipartisan task force, co-chaired by former Reps. Swift and Guy Vander Jagt, R, Mich. (1966-93), to develop an overhaul plan.

But they found little common ground. Democrats were leery of Republican efforts to enhance the role of political parties, a GOP strength. Republicans sought to curb PACs and regulate political activity by labor unions, two sources of Democratic strength.

The House and Senate also took differing positions on PACs. The Senate, whose members generally received less PAC money than House members, voted to disband PACs. The House passed language that only limited the amount candidates could take from PACs. In the end, conferees failed to reconcile their differences.

The House and Senate tried again in 1992 but again partisan differences could not be bridged. The Democratic-controlled Congress cleared legislation that set up separate systems for House and Senate races. The bill placed voluntary caps on overall spending and replaced limits on PAC and other contributions with public financing. Republicans objected, instead favoring an overall ban on PACs. President George Bush vetoed the measure, saying it unfairly favored Democrats.

The PAC controversy began to subside in the 1990s, as both parties mastered PAC fund-raising and a new form of campaign cash emerged: soft money. In contrast to "hard money," which is limited and goes to individual candidates, soft money is unlimited and can be used only for generic party-building activities—although in practice it often does help specific candidates through issue ads.

As the use of soft money grew in the 1990s, so did criticism.

In the 1992 federal election cycle, the Democratic and Republican campaign committees raised $36.3 million and $49.8 million in soft money, respectively. Those numbers grew to $123.9 million for Democrats and $138.2 million for Republicans in 1996. Today, political parties are on their way to a new soft money record.

In the first 15 months of this election cycle, Democratic and Republican party committees raised a combined $160.5 million, according to a study by the government watchdog group Common Cause. That is nearly double the $84.6 million raised during the first 15 months of the 1995-96 cycle.

The two parties received 140 soft money donations in single amounts of $100,000 or more during the first three months of 2000, according to Common Cause.

Among those contributing massive amounts of soft money this year was tobacco giant Philip Morris Companies, which gave gifts of $100,000 each in soft money to the Republican National Committee, the National Republican Congressional Committee and the

National Republican Senatorial Committee. On the Democratic side, telecomcomunications company SBC Communications Inc. gave the largest single soft money contribution of the year: $350,000 to the Democratic National Committee (DNC).

"We have come a long way from the days when the national parties represented their voters and acted as true grass-roots organizations," said Scott Harshbarger, president of Common Cause. "In today's soft money dominated system, the parties have become glorified mail-drops for special-interest money."

Companies that give large donations say they are merely participating in the democratic process. "No," said SBC spokesman Matthew Miller when asked if its donations are aimed at influencing public policy. "We are a major Fortune 500 firm, and as a major participant in the political process, our role is to give money not just to candidates but to political parties as well."

Miller said the large donation to the DNC was prompted by the Democratic convention being held this summer in Los Angeles, a major market for SBC.

"We want to be a good host to the Democratic Party when they have their convention in our city," Miller said. He added that SBC also gives to the GOP, and company contributions to both parties will likely even out by the end of the cycle.

Unreported Money

Although soft money has been the focus of recent campaign overhaul efforts, a new fundraising technique is emerging that some say could eclipse all other fund-raising controversies.

A growing number of political groups are forming the "527s." Such groups were originally expected to report their fund-raising and spending to the FEC. But as long as the groups do not expressly advocate the election or defeat of a specific candidate, they are not required to report anything. They can run ads attacking or praising a candidate; they can distribute voter guides condemning the political philosophy of candidates; and they can engage in other political activities that fall under the broad title of "issue advocacy"—all without having to abide by disclosure laws.

The use of issue ads has grown dramatically in recent years. A study by the Annenberg Public Policy Center of the University of Pennsylvania found that more than $114 million has been spent on or committed to issue ads so far this cycle. That is nearly equal to the amount spent on issue ads during the entire 1996 cycle. With six months to go until the elections, issue ad spending is expected to hit an all-time high, the study said.

The "527" groups that run issue ads can accept unlimited amounts of money from any source, including foreign governments. Because there are no public registration laws for such groups, their numbers and influence are incalculable.

The Center for Responsive Politics and Common Cause have so far compiled a list of more than a dozen "527" groups. They range ideologically from the far left to the far right. Several are affiliated with prominent special-interest groups, such as the Christian Coalition, the League of Conservation Voters and the Sierra Club. Others are independent groups, such as the Committee for New American Leadership, which was founded by former House Speaker Newt Gingrich, R-Ga. (1979-99), and seeks to cap taxes at 25 percent of income and enhance the United States' global role. The group uses the Internet and "other mechanisms for mobilizing voters so that candidates who support such issues will be elected to office," according to its Web site. Several "527s" are closely affiliated with current congressional leaders. ("527s," P. 1091)

Makinson of the Center for Responsive Politics calls "527s" dangerous, but officials who work with the groups defend their activities.

DeLay has worked closely with the Republican Majority Issues Committee, a "527" group that wants to spend $25 million on voter registration, voter turnout and issue ads this year to counter labor union activities in behalf of Democrats.

"527" groups "are legal," DeLay said. "They have been used by the left for many years." He mentioned a "527" group organized by the Sierra Club, an environmental group. "I am for full disclosure, but not for unilateral disarmament. We will continue to use legal organizations to express our point of view."

Another group, Saving America's Families Everyday (SAFE), is working to raise more than $1 million this year to conduct polls for the GOP. House Republican Conference Chairman J. C. Watts Jr. of Oklahoma is a leading fund-raiser for the group.

"We're playing by the rules as they are," said Tim Crawford, executive director of SAFE. "If they change the rules and say you need to disclose your donors, we wouldn't have a problem with that." Crawford added, however, that not having to disclose donors helps fund-raising. "Some donors don't want their names used so they're not pestered," he said.

Calls for Change

As Congress continues its attempts to change campaign fund-raising, even those who support an overhaul concede that there is no quick fix. "No matter what system you set up, someone is going to figure it out, and you will have to pass a new law," Swift said.

Ornstein said campaign finance overhaul advocates might eventually have to agree to raise certain limits to keep up with inflation. In today's dollars, the limit on individual contributions should be about triple the $1,000 set a quarter-century ago.

Given the brain power of lawyers and experts searching for loopholes, McCain said, no law will stand forever. "There will always be corruption in American politics," he said. "That's why there are cycles of reform throughout our history. If it's cleaned up, it will stay cleaned up for another 10 or 15 years or so, and then there will be another McCain and Feingold."

As Swift put it, Congress can always pass regulations, but "you can't enforce virtue."

Double Down: A Look At Soft Money Fund-Raising by Leadership PACs[9]

BY HOLLY BAILEY
CENTER FOR RESPONSIVE POLITICS, OCTOBER 30, 2000

Heading into the final week before Election Day, the battle for control of Congress has never been tighter, with Democrats and Republicans dead even in their quests to capture the controlling majority on Capitol Hill.

With that in mind, it shouldn't be surprising that a few members of Congress are chipping in a little extra to help their fellow comrades, especially where soft money is concerned.

According to newly-filed records with the Internal Revenue Service, roughly 25 political action committees affiliated with members of Congress have taken unlimited and previously undisclosed campaign checks, some totaling as high as $150,000 a pop.

Among those going the extra mile have been House Speaker Dennis Hastert, Sentate Majority Leader Trent Lott, House Majority Whip Tom DeLay and Sen. Edward Kennedy (D-Mass), all of whom have raised tens—in some cases, hundreds—of thousands of dollars in soft money from individuals and corporations via their leadership PACs, in addition to the money already reported to the Federal Election Commission.

This marks the first time such information had been available. Congress earlier this summer passed legislation requiring political groups filed under Section 527 of the federal tax code to disclose contributions over $200 and expenditures to the Internal Revenue Service, should they not already be filing the information with the FEC or on the state level.

The law was intended to close a much-exploited loophole in which innocuously named groups like Citizens for Better Medicare spent millions on issue ads and stealth campaigns aimed at influencing an election without disclosing their identity or finances. However, it hasn't been just the so-called special interests hiding behind the loophole.

A search of records filed over the last few weeks with the IRS shows that 18 committees with ties to members of Congress took in an estimated $2.9 million in soft money between July and Septem-

---

ber, the first period addressed by the new guidelines. Yet, that number is anything but final as the IRS continues to make reports public.

The top recipient of soft money dollars thus far has been the Majority Leader's Fund, a leadership PAC affiliated with Rep. Dick Armey (R-Texas). The fund, according to the IRS, took in roughly $581,000 in soft money contributions, including a $50,000 check from the NY-based financial firm Cerberus Partners. Enron, SBC Communications and Federal Express each contributed $25,000, but perhaps the most ironic disclosure was a pair of $12,500 checks from Charles and Sam Wyly, the Texas brothers who in part inspired Congress' crackdown on the 527 loophole.

Sam Wyly, who funded a series of issue ads blasting Sen. John McCain's environmental record during the GOP presidential primary, also contributed $20,000 to the American Dream Fund, a PAC affiliated with Rep. Henry Bonilla (R-Texas).

But that's nothing compared to the $150,000 check Amway's Rich DeVos sent to the Republican Majority Issues Committee, a nonprofit affiliated with DeLay. Among the committee's other contributors: Enron executives Kenneth Lay ($50,000) and Joseph Sutton ($25,000), Edward Atsinger of Salem Communications ($20,000) and the Anschultz Corp ($20,000). Investment icon Charles Schwab, meanwhile, contributed $25,000 to DeLay's leadership PAC, Americans for a Republican Majority.

Hastert's Keep Our Majority PAC reported a $100,000 check from construction equipment giant Caterpillar, while another $90,000 came from the Associated Builders and Contractors. AT&T chipped in $50,000. Lott's PAC, the New Republican Majority Fund, reported two major checks: $25,000 from Lodwrick Cook, co-chair of Global Crossing and $10,000 from SBC Communications.

House Republican Conference Chairman J. C. Watts (R-Okla) raised roughly $180,000 in soft money through two committees: his American Renewal PAC and Saving America's Families Everyday (SAFE), a separate non-profit that he chairs. Among his donors: Daniel Snyder, owner of the Washington Redskins, who gave $10,000; Coca Cola ($10,000); and the National Rifle Association ($10,000).

The NRA also contributed $12,500 in soft money to Sen. Larry Craig (R-Idaho) via his PAC, Alliance for the West and $15,000 to Mainstream America PAC, affiliated with Sen. Sam Brownback (R-Kan).

But it's not just Republicans who have been raking in the soft money. Rep. Martin Frost (D-Texas) raised $256,800 via his PAC, the Lone Star Fund, thanks to checks from SBC Communications ($12,500), Microsoft (an in-kind gift of $5,500), Texas Utilities Corp ($25,000) and Enron ($10,000).

Kennedy's Committee for a Democratic Majority reported $108,164 in soft money checks from roughly a dozen people, including $45,000 from five members of the Wolfington Family–the faces behind Carey International, a DC-based chauffeured vehicle service company. Sen. Harry Reid (D-Nev), through his Searchlight Leadership Fund, reported a $50,000 check from the Washington Group International, a construction and engineering firm, while DASHPAC, affiliated with Senate Minority Leader Tom Daschle, reported several $10,000 checks, including one from the Association of Trial Lawyers of America.

Fund-raising by Committees Affiliated with Members of Congress 1999-2000

Committee	Total Soft Money Raised	Total Hard Money Raised	Affiliate
Alliance for the West	$75,950	$69,654	Larry E. Craig (R-Idaho)
American Dream PAC	$60,750	$85,327	Henry Bonilla (R-Texas)
American Renewal PAC	$117,750	$318,515	J.C. Watts (R-Okla)
Americans for a Republican Majority	$94,500	$2,022,468	Tom DeLay (R-Texas)
Citizens for a Competitive America	$65,500	$20,750	Ernest F. Hollings (D-SC)
Committee for a Democratic Majority	$108,164	$347,563	Edward M. Kennedy (D-Mass)
DASHPAC	$84,500	$1,055,533	Tom Daschle (D-SD)
Keep Our Majority PAC	$549,000	$585,164	Dennis Hastert (R-Ill)
Lone Star Fund	$256,800	$316,325	Martin Frost (D-Texas)
Mainstream America PAC	$43,750	$174,209	John B. Breaux (D-La)
Majority Leader's Fund	$581,474	$866,240	Dick Armey (R-Texas)
New Republican Majority Fund	$62,000	$1,555,169	Trent Lott (R-Miss)
Pioneer PAC	$13,000	$150,233	John R. Kasich (R-Ohio)
Republican Majority Issues Committee	$482,240	$0	Tom DeLay (R-Texas)
Restore America PAC	$43,000	$36,697	Sam Brownback (R-Kan)
Sandhills PAC	$6,000	$183,619	Chuck Hagel (R-Neb)
Saving Americas Families Everyday (SAFE)	$61,000	$0	J.C. Watts (R-Okla)
Searchlight Leadership Fund	$156,500	$247,477	Harry Reid (D-Nev)

III. The Debate Over Campaign Finance Reform

Editor's Introduction

I n spite of efforts to enact campaign finance reform, there are many who question the need for spending limits. Others question reform on the basis of the First Amendment to the U.S. Constitution and equate campaign contributions with free speech. Proponents of reform argue that corporations and special interest groups that contribute substantially to political campaigns expect something in return—and they are seldom disappointed. The debate over campaign finance reform reveals that there are no simple remedies for the corruption that has frustrated and alienated so many American citizens from the electoral process. Section III features a representative selection of the perspectives of those on both sides of the issue.

In "The Reform Quandary" Jeremy Lehrer provides an introduction to the key issues in the debate, including claims that campaign finance reform may violate the First Amendment to the Constitution. The second article, "One Cheer for Soft Money" by Steven E. Schier, questions the assertion made by Senator John McCain and others that soft money equals corruption. Schier contends that the appearance of corruption created by the prevalence of such contributions is a price that we should be willing to pay to keep the two major political parties strong. He suggests placing a cap on soft money, rather than eliminating it altogether.

Bob Schiff, writing for *The Progressive*, refutes the constitutional objection to reform and offers examples of instances in which political contributions influenced policy, such as the massive effort made by the wealthy insurance industry to stop President Clinton's proposals for health care reform. This is followed by an article by Bradley A. Smith, for *USA Today*, which challenges the widely held notion that campaign spending is out of control. Smith points out that money allows a candidate to reach a greater number of potential voters, and he further reminds us that outspending a political opponent does not necessarily guarantee victory. According to this article, campaign finance reform favors incumbents, elite members of the media, lobbying groups, and wealthy candidates.

In "Campaign Primer's First Lesson: Cash Flows From Contacts," Senator Robert G. Torricelli provides *Washington Post* writer Guy Gugliotta with a detailed description of the process by which he raised the money for his successful senate campaign in 1996. The article which follows, "Free Money," by *Reason* commentator James V. DeLong, considers the debate over soft money in the 2000 election. DeLong tracks the rising cost of elections, as well as key Supreme Court decisions on campaign finance, and defends soft money spending as a way for challengers to defeat incumbent opponents. Like Smith, DeLong contends that spending limits favor incumbents, while he also argues that campaign finance reform hinders free speech. This article also looks at flaws in existing campaign finance regulations and questions the assumption that too much is spent on political campaigns.

Next, Milton S. Gwirtzman discusses ways in which the Supreme Court has hindered efforts toward campaign finance reform. His article, "A Look At . . . Roadblocks to Campaign Reform," claims that both the Supreme Court and political candidates have ignored the rising disgust among voters, and that the court has proven itself to be out of touch with the reality of contemporary campaigning. In the final article in this section, "The First Step in Campaign Finance Reform: Fix the FEC," economist and former Reform Party vice-presidential candidate Pat Choate suggests that, for reform to occur, the FEC must be empowered to enforce campaign finance regulations and released from the stranglehold of the U.S. Congress.

The Reform Quandary[1]

By Jeremy Lehrer
Human Rights, Winter 1998

In June of 1997, a prominent elected official wrote to the Federal Election Commission appealing for reform of the country's campaign finance system: "The rules governing our system of financing Federal election campaigns are sorely out of date. Enacted more than two decades ago when election campaigns were much less expensive, the rules have been overtaken by dramatic changes in the nature and cost of campaigns and the accompanying flood of money."

The politician, of course, was none other than William J. Clinton, the 42nd president of the United States, and the appeal for change is one often made by politicians and advocates as campaign finance abuses escalate and as the public begins to wonder whether elected officials are accountable to their constituencies or to large donors. Advocates of reform argue that the current system has distorted the process to such an extent that special interests dominate Congress and that there are no real choices on election day.

Since government, politics, and economics are so intrinsically linked, money and politics will be forever wedded. As Micah Sifry, a senior analyst for Public Campaign, a nonprofit organization advocating campaign finance reform, observes, "You cannot legislate money out of politics."

Even so, the history of reform goes to the end of the 19th century, when the Pendleton Act was passed to ensure that government employees would not solicit funds for political parties on government property. Vice President Al Gore is quite familiar with this particular statute, since he has been accused of violating the Pendleton Act when he called donors from the White House. Another piece of reform legislation, the Corrupt Practices Act of 1907, was signed into law during the tenure of President Theodore Roosevelt (his second term) and was designed to prohibit corporations from financing congressional and presidential elections. (The first President Roosevelt, whom President Clinton has evoked more than once, had money problems of his own that provided impetus for the reform.)

---

1. Article by Jeremy Lehrer from *Human Rights*. Copyright © American Bar Association. Reprinted with permission.

More recently, comprehensive campaign finance reform legislation was passed in 1974 following revelations of corruption and payback that occurred during the Nixon administration. As initially passed by Congress, the legislation, known as the Federal Election Campaign Act (FECA), limited contributions to candidates and imposed spending limits on candidates running for office. In one of the legislation's most significant reforms, the 1974 Act provided for matching public funds during presidential primaries and public financing during the general elections in an attempt to liberate presidential candidates from private money and special interests. The presidential subsidies are funded by a checkoff on income tax forms. If a candidate raises a certain amount of money and voluntarily agrees to honor spending limits, the candidate is eligible for public matching payments during the presidential primaries.

While Buckley sets the tone for the current debate, there are challenges to the ruling from both sides of the reform divide.

In *Buckley v. Valeo*, 424 U.S. 1, 19 (1976), the Supreme Court overturned sections of FECA while it upheld other parts. The Court concluded in the 1976 ruling that mandatory spending limits were unconstitutional and a violation of a candidate's First Amendment right to free speech. However, the Justices ruled that contribution limits were an acceptable means of undermining corruption and added that regulatory systems were constitutional only so long as they were voluntary. Independent expenditures on behalf of a candidate and a candidate's spending of personal funds fell under the realm of protected free speech.

While *Buckley* sets the tone for the current debate, there are challenges to the ruling from both sides of the reform divide. As Donald Simon, the executive vice president and general counsel of Common Cause, notes, "Those who oppose regulation believe that *Buckley* permits too much regulation and those who support regulation believe that *Buckley* permits too little."

Supporters of increased regulation look no farther than the last presidential election, when large amounts of "soft money" were raised by both political parties, funneled to state party and other organizations, and used to fund campaign commercials, a tactic forbidden by current campaign legislation. "Soft money" is money given to political parties that is not subject to contribution limitations imposed on individual candidates. The money is intended to be used for only party building activities such as get-out-the-vote drives and voter registration initiatives sanctioned by a 1979 amendment to the FECA legislation. But since 1988—observers cite the Dukakis campaign as the culprit in the development—soft money has been used to circumvent limits on contributions and spending.

According to Common Cause, in the 1996 election cycle, Democrats raised $124 million in soft money and Republicans raised $138 million. In the first six months of 1997 up until June 30, the Democrats raised over $11 million, and the Republicans raised more than $23 million, more than twice that raised during the same period in 1993. Though the 1979 amendment states that these contributions cannot be spent in support of specific candidates unless the expenditures comply with limits, they were nevertheless used in the last election to do just that. Among other issues, advocacy organizations have charged that the Federal Election Commission, the organization created to enforce federal election law, has failed to fulfill its mandate. Indeed, in a 1987 court ruling, *Common Cause v. Federal Election Commission*, a federal court found that the FEC's approach to regulating soft money failed to reflect the intent of the law.

Though many voices are calling for reform, the effort to achieve it is an exercise in negotiating a legal mine field. Some commentators have noted that campaign finance reform brings First Amendment values into conflict with values of democracy and equality. Bradley Smith, an associate professor at Capital University Law School in Columbus, Ohio, has written articles about campaign finance reform and its First Amendment implications for the *Wall Street Journal* and the *Yale Law Journal*. Smith is an ardent supporter of the *Buckley* position that political spending amounts to speech protected by the First Amendment and argues that current reform proposals contain provisions that impinge on free speech.

"Most of the things that are being proposed are I think both unwise policy and unconstitutional as a matter of First Amendment law," he says.

The ACLU holds a similar position, though there has been some internal debate regarding the organization's position on campaign finance reform. The ACLU supports public financing but opposes contribution limits, and though *Buckley* allows voluntary compliance with spending limits, the ACLU opposes these limits and has been participating in litigation to challenge them. As Laura Murphy, the director of the ACLU's Washington, D.C., office, explains, "There are always unique circumstances where a spending limit becomes arbitrary."

Beyond spending limits, issue ads are another contentious subject in the campaign finance reform debate. Paid for by organizations or individuals, issue ads are intended to focus on a political or legislative issue without advocating the defeat or election of a particular candidate. Supporters of issue ads, like Bradley Smith, claim that the *Buckley* decision establishes a clear allowance, and Smith adds that "talking about politics requires people to use the names of candidates and to talk about them in the context of issues." Critics maintain that issue ads sometimes cross the line into express advocacy without being subject to the disclosure required of campaign advertisements. While reformers appeal for some level of disclosure for issue ads, opponents such as Murphy argue that this could have "a chilling effect on free speech."

"There may be forms of disclosure that are not as burdensome as some others," says Murphy. "But the forms of issue disclosure that are in the prevailing or the most prominent campaign finance reform proposals are not acceptable to the ACLU."

Specific proposals to refine the current campaign financing system range from those who would like to see the system fully financed by public funds to those who would like to see the current system entirely deregulated.

Donald Simon would like to see a refined approach that would distinguish between issue ads and express advocacy but acknowledges that there are "substantial constitutional questions about how to deal with that problem." The problem, as Simon sees it, is how to draw a line between campaign ads, which are subject to regulation, and issue ads, which are not. "The line that is in place today is a clear line but it's also clearly the wrong line because it allows ads that are unquestionably campaign ads to escape regulation."

Specific proposals to refine the current campaign financing system range from those who would like to see the system fully financed by public funds to those who would like to see the current system entirely deregulated.

McCain-Feingold, also known as the Bipartisan Campaign Reform Act of 1997, is a reform bill that sought to solve a number of problems in the current campaign finance system. Among other things, McCain-Feingold had provisions for banning soft money, distinguishing between issue ads and express advocacy, providing greater public disclosure, and codifying the Supreme Court's *Beck* decision, a ruling that stated that workers could not be forced to pay dues or fees to subsidize union activity unrelated to collective bargaining. Because of a Republican filibuster, voting on McCain-Feingold did not occur in 1997. However, due to pressure by Democrats and by the Senate Governmental Affairs Committee hearings on campaign finance abuses, the bill will be brought again to the Senate floor in March 1998. And there seems to be parallel pressure in the House to achieve some level of reform.

On another end of the spectrum is legislation introduced by Representative John Doolittle, a California Republican, which would eliminate restrictions on contributions and spending but require electronic disclosure of donations within 24 hours. This legislation has the support of those who would like to deregulate the campaign finance system entirely as well as legal scholars who argue that limits on contributions and spending actually end up benefiting incumbents, who have significant fund-raising and organizational advantages over their challengers.

While campaign finance reform stalls at the federal level, some states have successfully passed campaign finance reform legislation.

From some corners, there have even been rumblings and suggestions that a constitutional amendment should be made that would limit campaign spending. The prospect of a campaign finance amendment has reformers on both sides of the divide worried that core political speech would be curtailed. But since it would be difficult if not impossible to pass such an amendment, Micah Sifry argues that the proposal is a red herring, coverage for politicians who don't really want to see reform of the system.

While campaign finance reform stalls at the federal level, some states have successfully passed campaign finance reform legislation. In 1996, voters in Maine passed a ballot initiative that provided full public financing to candidates, and Public Campaign, led by Ellen Miller, a former executive director of the Center for Responsive Politics, supports this system as a model for reform on a wider level; Kerry-Wellstone, another reform proposal presented in the Senate, is based on the Maine reform bill.

The Maine Clean Elections Act provides full public financing to candidates who accept no private money and agree to abide by spending limits. Candidates qualify for the financing by initially collecting a threshold number of $5 donations to demonstrate broad support among constituents. If a candidate accepts private funds at any time, the offender is subject to stiff penalties that include forfeiting, returning the grant, and paying fines.

Regarding the Maine system, Sifry observes that a full public financing arrangement frees candidates from commitments that develop when accepting money from large contributors.

"If the candidate has an alternative source of financing that essentially frees them in the first place from needing to raise any money then in effect you're rewarding them for virtuous behavior rather than trying to coerce them away from what you think of as less than virtuous behavior," he says. "There will still be 'old-fashioned,' privately financed candidates, and there will still be money in politics, you can't get rid of it. But what finally we will have is a choice between candidates who are beholden to special interest donors and candidates who are beholden to nobody."

Bradley Smith argues that in the public financing scenario, candidates will be beholden to other groups, such as the media and academia, that would end up wielding greater influence if donors are removed from the political equation. "I reject this sort of notion that money is in some ways an illegitimate source of power but being a television broadcaster is legitimate. Being an academic is legitimate but donating $10,000 is not."

Broadcasters wield influence in many ways, and some campaign finance reform advocates have suggested that purchases of television time are one of the most pernicious influences on modern campaigns. Because television time costs so much money, candidates are forced to raise the inordinate amounts of money that have become commonplace in electoral drives. To eliminate the need for these sums of money, reformers have suggested that television stations provide free or reduced air time to candidates running for office.

In addition to objections from broadcasters that do not want to lose advertising revenue, the free TV proposal raises objections from First Amendment advocates who argue that it is an imposition on free speech and an unconstitutional "taking." Laura Murphy, of the ACLU, contends that there are "compelled speech issues" involved with the proposal and supports instead a system of publicly financed vouchers that would enable candidates to purchase advertisements in media ranging from television to newspapers. Micah Sifry, of Public Campaign, argues that the television stations are obligated to give something back to the public in return for using the public airwaves and notes that stations are also required to provide a certain amount of children's educational and public service programming.

Advocates of free TV seem to agree that the government missed out on an opportunity to require free air time for candidates when the government essentially gave away additional sections of the broadcast spectrum earlier this year in preparation for the transition to digital television. The additional spectrum was given away to broadcasters without requiring them to give back a single red cent or even a programming concession, though the spectrum's value was estimated as close to $70 billion.

The broadcast spectrum giveaway gets back to an idea about the value of campaign donations and the lucrative payback industries can reap if the legislative wind blows in the right direction. While not necessarily a quid pro quo, donors have certainly benefited from certain aspects of legislation or policy that might otherwise have benefited the public good. The spectrum's estimated value of $70 billion is a financial leviathan compared to the Mickey Mouse millions that communications and entertainment companies donated to the major parties over the course of the last election cycle. Don Simon observes, "That's why campaign contributions are viewed as investments, and they're viewed as good investments."

Investments or not, campaign finance reform remains a thorny issue that will undoubtedly stir heated debate for some time to come.

One Cheer for Soft Money[2]

By Steven E. Schier
Washington Monthly, July/August 2000

To listen to John McCain, you'd think that the fate of the republic hinges on the immediate ban of soft money contributions to political parties. His Web page, *www.itsyourcountry.com*, boldly asserts: "Ban soft money and your voice will be heard in Washington again." Why? "Without reining in soft money and reducing the role of money in politics, we will never have a government that works as hard for the average American as it does for the special interests."

Translation: national government is corrupt largely because of soft money and by clamping down on soft money, political corruption will shrivel. It's a simple and appealing formula. As with most such formulas, however, it misreads reality and promises more than it can deliver. Though we do need to address any possible corruption resulting from campaign contributions, we need to do it in a way that doesn't damage the ability of our already-weak political parties to add some coherence to America's peculiarly complex, candidate-centered politics.

The Hard Goods on Soft Money

Soft money refers to unlimited contributions directly from corporations, unions, and individuals to party committees. A series of Congressional amendments and Federal Election Commission rulings in the 1970s and 1980s permitted political parties to raise unlimited funds for "election related activities" by state and local parties. These monies, held in "nonfederal" accounts, are not subject to the "hard money" limits of the funds in "federal" accounts. Hard money limits cap annual individual contributions at $25,000. They require interest groups to contribute to candidates and parties through regulated Political Action Committees at a maximum rate of $5,000 per candidate per (primary or general) election and limit individual contributions to $1,000 per candidate per election. Though wealthy individuals, corporations, and unions are thus sharply limited in their hard money contributions, the sky is the contribution limit with soft money.

---

2. Reprinted with permission from *The Washington Monthly.* Copyright by The Washington Monthly Company, 1611 Connecticut Ave., N.W., Washington, DC 20009 (202) 462-0128. Web site: *www.washingtonmonthly.com.*

Since 1980 the parties' national committees and their House and Senate campaign committees have raised increasingly mammoth amounts of soft money, cresting at $262 million in 1996 and $250 million in 1998. Where does all of this money go? Originally, soft money was to be spent on grassroots campaigning by state and local parties for brochures, door knocking, and get-out-the-vote efforts.

The real explosion in soft money fund-raising occurred after a 1995 Federal Election Commission ruling that permitted the parties to spend soft money on "issue advocacy" advertising, an obscure government action that had huge consequences. Though issue-advocacy advertising legally cannot expressly advocate the election or defeat of a candidate, it can link candidates to issues in a way that supports or opposes their election. What is express advocacy? The FEC defined it as any communication that uses phrases like "vote for," "vote against," "elect," or "defeat," and "can have no other reasonable meaning than to urge the election or defeat of one or more clearly identified candidates." Creative campaign minds found all sorts of ways around those restrictions in 1996. The race for soft money to fund issue-advocacy advertising had begun.

The real lesson for candidates from the Clinton experience in 1996 is that soft-money spending works.

The campaign finance scandals afflicting the Clinton presidency in recent years have involved raising soft money from dubious, often overseas sources in large amounts. But the real lesson for candidates from the Clinton experience in 1996 is that soft money spending works. The Democratic party committees spent over $46.5 million on soft-money-funded ads aiding Clinton's re-election in 1996, many of which appeared early in the election year before Dole and the Republicans were able to respond (they eventually did, but with a comparatively meager $18 million in soft money ads).

Soft money can spell the difference between victory and defeat, as the 1998 Kentucky Senate race revealed. Pitting two House incumbents, Democrat Scotty Baesler and Republican Jim Bunning, against each other, the race featured an orgy of soft money spending by the state parties. Though Baesler began the fall campaign with a double-digit lead over Bunning, he was short on funds after winning a competitive primary. Bunning was assisted by over $1.5 million worth of ads paid for by the Kentucky Republican Party, raised with the help of Republican Sen. Mitch McConnell, an outspoken defender of soft money. One GOP soft money ad attacked Baesler for supporting NAFTA, concluding with a stereotypical Mexican saying, "Muchas Gracias, Senor Baesler." The state Democratic Party could only spend one-third of the Republican total for ads. The money disparity helped Bunning earn a narrow victory in November.

What's Bad About Soft Money?

McCain and his fellow reformers have some good arguments against the current soft money regime. It's not wise to allow corporations and unions to give unlimited amounts to parties. Large corporations give huge amounts to parties to secure or defend favorable governmental treatment. The publicly owned digital television spectrum was recently distributed for free to television broadcasters, who have given $5 million in soft money in recent years. Agribusiness companies have given over $4.5 million in soft money in recent years, helping to maintain federal ethanol subsidies worth $500 million annually. Even if these actions aren't out-and-out bribes, they certainly present an "appearance of corruption" to many citizens.

In addition to bad appearances, the explosion of soft money advertising has increased the "clutter" of messages besieging voters during election campaigns. Political scientist David Magelby, in a recent book on the impact of soft-money and issue-advocacy advertising in the 1998 elections, concludes that in competitive House and Senate races, voters are "inundated" with communications about the candidates and that "the negative tone of many of the noncandidate ads has the potential to reinforce alienation and cynicism among voters." In several states, party ads were more negative than those run by candidate campaigns.

So if soft money contributes to at least the appearance of corruption in national politics, confuses and alienates voters, we should get rid of it, right? That is certainly the conventional wisdom about campaign finance reform in many Washington circles. But it's not entirely correct. We need to keep parties well-funded in some form to ensure they don't have their electoral role greatly diminished. Why? Because, despite the clutter, there are some good arguments for party-based election advertising. Our elections can survive the onset of message clutter, but they can't prosper without robust national parties at the center of the campaigns.

The Virtues of Soft Money

The attack on soft money is appropriately an attack on corruption, but it's also an attack on political parties themselves. Throughout American history, political parties have performed vital services for our democracy. America would benefit from stronger parties, for three reasons. First, strong parties bring people into politics. By distilling the choice among a variety of candidates to a selection between one of two partisan "teams," parties lower information costs for voters, thus encouraging those with less education and less income to vote. In the twentieth century, as ballots have become more complex, it has become harder for many voters to sort their way through the increasing amount of information needed to make an informed decision.

The growing trend of recent decades has been toward more personalism in politics, dominated by candidates selling themselves, not a common party platform. Though Congress is more partisan lately because of the close competitive balance between the parties, the public has turned away from political parties. Political scientist Marvin Wattenberg has found that steadily more members of the public have no views at all about political parties and find them less and less relevant to politics. Accordingly, candidates sell themselves as individuals. Just ask yourself when was the last time you saw a party label prominently displayed in a candidate's general election TV or radio ads? Parties have all but disappeared from candidate communication with general election voters because candidates find the party label less useful in rounding up support.

As support for parties and turnout in elections has declined, interest-group membership has grown.

This sort of politics occurs in Latin American countries such as Peru and Venezuela, where presidents Fujimori and Chavez appeal to the masses first. In both countries, personalism has weakened parties and democracy. Though America is far from the instability of Peru and Venezuela, it shares with them a pattern of declining voter participation and disengagement of large segments of the population from politics. The 49 percent turnout in the 1996 U.S. presidential election was the lowest since 1924, shortly after women got the vote. The 36 percent turnout in the 1998 midterm election was the lowest since the 1942 midterm, which occurred in the middle of a world war.

Second, strong parties can shield lawmakers from the very special-interest influence that many accuse them of surrendering to. As support for parties and turnout in elections has declined, interest-group membership has grown. Now, the proportion of Americans who are interest group members far exceeds the ranks of strong party identifiers. A 1990 survey conducted for the American Society of Association Executives estimated that 70 percent of the public are members of associations, while the number of strong partisans hovers around 30 percent.

As interests grew in numbers and strength in recent decades, lawmakers became more responsive to them. The number of groups listed in the Encyclopedia of Associations mushroomed from 5,000 in 1956 to 23,000 by 1996 and a record number of lobbyists now ply their trade in Washington. From the National Federation of Independent Businesses on the right to the American Association of Retired Persons on the left, national government is beset by hundreds of well-funded, effective, and insistent interest groups. With their resources of campaign money, hired analysts, and memberships that vote, their clout has never been greater.

This cacophony of interests has its costs. Proliferating interest groups do not produce accountable government the way party-based elections can. Worldwide, nations with weak party systems have low participation in elections. Meager electoral participation plays into the hands of organized special interests. In America, these special interests are highly skilled in the art of activating their members to vote and lobby. And with fewer other voters, such groups have a larger voice in electoral outcomes. You need look no farther than the success of Christian conservative groups in promoting the Republican triumph in the 1994 elections to see how well-organized interest groups benefit when others stay home.

Political scientist Robert Putnam correctly argues that accountability to a broad set of interests can only result from heavy electoral participation that exerts influence over the behavior of elected officials. Strong party systems have a global record of facilitating that participation. In America's weak party system, low participation reduces the accountability of those we elect to broad, common interests and enhances their accountability to the narrower set of organized interest groups that help get their favorite candidates elected.

Third, strong and stable parties are essential to the stability of democracy itself. Most of the world's democracies that have survived 25 years or more have had stable party systems with a low number of parties. In most of these nations, parties dominate elections and the operation of government. Many such democracies (and most of the European ones) allow voters to vote only for parties, instead of individual candidates, in elections and have parliamentary systems in which parties gain control of the legislative and executive branches and rule as highly disciplined teams. American parties, in contrast, are a rag-tag assemblage of electoral individualists.

Walter Dean Burnham of the University of Texas summarizes what parties can do for us: "Political parties, with all their well-known human and structural shortcomings, are the only devices thus far invented by the wit of Western man that can, with some effectiveness, generate countervailing collective power on behalf of the many individually powerless against the relatively few who are individually or organizationally powerful." Parties are the best available means for linking majority preferences with governmental action because they help to simplify and clarify voting choices.

Choosing between two teams rather than among a plethora of individual candidates makes it easier for more citizens to cast an informed vote. That's one major reason why turnout in just about every other constitutional democracy is well above that of the United States.

To restore this vital party function, we need to make our elections more about parties and their philosophies and less about individual candidates and their personalities. Giving parties more

---

Soft-money contributions must be limited to prevent corruption, but preserved to prevent further party decline.

---

resources with which to do this requires that we not diminish their role in national elections, but rather ensure that they are well funded in ways that minimize apparent or actual corruption.

By encouraging contributions to parties instead of to individual candidates, we can actually limit corruption in American politics. The likelihood of a quid-pro-quo is always greater if the money goes directly to a candidate. By sending money to the parties, we create a "buffer" between campaign contributions and the government officials those contributions seek to influence. The trick is to keep the money from arriving in such large quantities to parties that the buffer virtually disappears, as it has at present.

Reforms to Help the Parties

We need to take several steps to restore parties to a central role in American politics. First, soft-money contributions must be limited to prevent corruption, but preserved to prevent further party decline. A desirable alternative to the McCain-Feingold ban on soft money lies in a bill sponsored by Sens. Bob Kerrey (D) and Chuck Hagel (R) of Nebraska. Their bill caps soft-money contributions at $60,000 per year and indexes hard-money limits for inflation since 1974, effectively tripling them. The soft-money cap will greatly reduce the likelihood of corruption through soft money and the higher hard-money limits will permit larger hard-money contributions to parties.

Second, we need to keep the hard-money individual and PAC contribution limits to candidates low, while raising them considerably for political parties. Hard-money limits are enforced and recorded by the Federal Election Commission. Currently, individuals can only give a maximum of $20,000 a year to political parties. That limit should be raised to $50,000, while keeping the individual contribution limits to PACs and directly to candidates at $1,000. This will cause more funds to flow to parties, reducing the power of narrow interests in elections and curbing the appearance (and, at times, reality) of corruption linked to direct contributions from PACs to candidates. Even with higher hard-money contribution limits for parties, the Kerry-Hagel cap on soft-money contributions will prevent the "megacontributions" from unions and corporations to parties that plague our current politics.

Third, to make parties more central to campaigns, we need to allocate large blocks of free airtime to state and national parties for them to use to boost their candidates for national office. This can be a remarkably effective cure for electoral individualism. Campaigns are cash-intensive because of the need to buy TV ads, so giving parties power over ads really hits candidates where they live, making soft-money contributions integral to their success. To make parties more important, the blocks of time allocated to them need to be large. State parties could get one hour for each House candidate they field and two or more hours (pro-rated based on the ratio of Senators to Representatives) for their Senate candidates. National parties each need several hours of network time during the fall presidential campaigns.

Fourth, to weaken the role of interest groups in campaigns, we should ban corporations and unions from direct issue-advocacy electioneering. Those issue-advocacy ads that flood our airwaves during fall elections come straight from corporate and union treasuries, confusing voters and empowering narrow interests at the expense of parties. Such ads seek to aid particular candidates, evading laws passed by Congress that ban corporate contributions to candidates from corporations (in 1907) and unions (in 1947). Courts have upheld contribution bans in the past, so a legislative ban on issue-advocacy ads by such interests might well pass constitutional muster. We need to invite the Supreme Court to reverse *Buckley v. Valeo* on this point.

Fifth, the First Amendment does give individuals the right to run issue ads during campaigns, but the public should have the right to know who is doing the spending. It is difficult to imagine a narrower political interest than a single millionaire or a few wealthy individuals. Elections should involve large, strong parties with broad concerns, not a small number of rich folks with a particular agenda. If we cannot ban that advertising, we can at least strengthen disclosure laws to make it immediately clear who's bought the ads.

These changes will be weak tea for many campaign-finance reformers. Many would like to remove private money from elections completely, or equalize the spending of campaign money through government regulation. Aside from the political improbability of

such reforms, such changes would create more problems than they would solve. Figuring out how to equalize expression in campaigns between often little-known challengers and incumbents is an impossible task, and the Supreme Court in *Buckley v. Valeo* explicitly rejected governmental regulation to equalize campaign expression on first amendment grounds. Accordingly, any public financing plan would have to be voluntary (as is presidential campaign finance now). New state public financing laws, recently adopted in Maine and Vermont, however, give all the money directly to candidates and sharply restrict the funds parties can raise to influence elections. That is moving in the wrong direction. Instead of creating "a government that works as hard for the average American as it does for the special interests," as John McCain

---

Political parties may be part of the problem with electoral politics, but properly reviving them is very much part of the solution.

---

desires, these laws have diminished the electoral power of political parties, the institutions with the best worldwide record of stimulating turnout in elections.

The Maine and Vermont laws reveal an unpleasant truth about many campaign-finance reformers. Like the progressive movement of the early 20th century, they are aggressively anti-party. The progressives pushed through a variety of reforms that drastically curtailed the power of parties in American politics—the direct primary, personal voter registration, and the end of patronage hiring. As party power shrank, elections increasingly became contests between multitudes of individual candidates instead of between two parties. The electoral world became more indecipherable to more Americans. Guess what? Voting turnout dropped. And it's still remarkably low. During the partisan era of 100 years ago, turnouts of 75 percent were common in presidential elections, far above today's miserable levels, and involving a far less educated electorate than today's voters. Clearly, parties did something right. It's time to give them another chance.

Political parties may be part of the problem with electoral politics, but properly reviving them is very much part of the solution. We need to roll back corrupt practices while strengthening parties. Campaign-finance reformers need to understand that if they want robust campaigns and high turnout, they need to learn how to love political parties, not destroy them.

"The First Amendment Is Not a Stop Sign Against Reform"[3]

By Bob Schiff
The Progressive, December 1997

Campaign-finance scandals dominate the headlines. Public sentiment for reform is at its highest level since the Watergate era. Yet it
seems like the opposition to reform this year is bolder, and the odds
are getting longer. Even the McCain-Feingold bill, which many
reformers characterize as only a weak first step, faces heated and
determined opposition. Free marketeers aligned with the ACLU and
the Christian Right denounce attempts to reform the loophole-rid-
den, corruption-breeding system we now live with as attacks on the
sacred right of free speech.

It is no longer laughable in Congress to talk about getting rid of all
limits on campaign contributions. "The reforms enacted after
Watergate failed," critics say. "Let's just get rid of all restrictions,
disclose everything, and let the public decide." That such a proposal
gets a respectful hearing in Congress and on the editorial pages of
major dailies shows how far the debate has moved.

Now, more than ever, progressives need to make federal campaign-finance reform a priority. And while it is important to keep
long-term goals in mind, incremental solutions may offer our best
chance to make progress toward more sweeping change. Giving up
altogether is simply not an option, unless we don't care that the
public thinks Congress is up for auction, that voter turnout is at an
all-time low, and that corporate money drowns out the voices of
average people both in the legislature and on the campaign trail.

The simple reason why we need campaign-finance reform is that
money influences policy.

The players are different, the legislative issues come and go. But
the one constant in our political system is the need for money. Lots
of it. Candidate and party spending in the 1996 elections topped $2
billion. Hundreds of millions more were spent in unreported "issue
ads." The constant search for funding to run campaigns costs us
dearly. Candidates and elected officials spend inordinate amounts of

---

time raising money, and the pressure to cross the line into improper or even illegal activity can test the resolve of even the most ethical politicians.

It would be one thing if the people with big money to spend on elections were merely civic-minded or disinterested rich people, or even just wealthy ideologues from across the political spectrum, but they're not. Nor does a broad cross-section of the public make political contributions. Less than one-third of 1 percent of the population gave contributions totaling more than $200 in the 1996 election. A huge proportion of the campaign cash that politicians raise comes from business interests, giving them special access to and influence over the legislative process.

Take two major policy debates of the last two Congresses: health care and the new telecommunications law.

Remember the Clinton plan? Thirty-seven million Americans with no insurance? Harry and Louise? The Democrats squabbled, the Republicans obstructed, and the legislation imploded.

During the ill-fated health-care debate, campaign money flowed freely from those with an economic interest in shaping the legislation. According to the Center for Responsive Politics, individuals and PACs associated with the health industry (including doctors, hospitals, nursing homes, HMOs, and drug companies) made more than $37 million in contributions to candidates, split evenly between Democrats and Republicans. The American Medical Association alone contributed more than $2.5 million. At least sixty members of Congress who sat on one of the five committees with jurisdiction over the healthcare legislation received more than $50,000 in contributions from these health industry PACs and individuals.

In the end, opponents of reform won. Today, the number of uninsured Americans is more than forty million, and the corporatization of our health-care system continues unabated.

Fast-forward to the next Congress. The Republicans are in control and undertaking a massive rewrite of the telecommunications laws. A titanic struggle ensues among the Baby Bells, the long-distance phone companies, and the cable TV companies that want to compete for each other's business. The money flows again: According to the Center for Responsive Politics, in the 1996 election cycle the cable companies contributed more than $2 million to candidates and parties, the long-distance companies gave nearly $4 million, and the Baby Bells coughed up an astonishing $6.2 million.

As a result of that fight, consumers found themselves out in the cold. Cable rates went up, and the networks got an enormous government giveaway: The whole digital television spectrum is now theirs for free.

It is not just the colossal struggles of big-money interests on major legislative issues that show the need for reform. Tax loopholes and corporate-welfare giveaways manage to find their way into legislation with little or no public discussion.

We're all now familiar with the $50 billion tax break that Senate Majority Leader Trent Lott, Republican of Mississippi, and House Speaker Newt Gingrich, Republican of Georgia, engineered for the tobacco companies. When that deal was exposed, the public outcry forced Congress to repeal it. Tobacco companies' soft-money contributions of $5.7 million to the Republican Party in 1996 and another $1.6 million in the first six months of this year surely greased the wheels for that effort to slip one by us.

> *During the ill-fated health-care debate, campaign money flowed freely from those with an economic interest in shaping the legislation.*

And how about the $280 million special tax break for Amway Corporation? Amway Chairman Richard DeVos and his wife have already contributed $1 million in soft money to the Republican party this year. That follows on the heels of the $315,000 that Amway gave to the Republicans in the 1996 cycle, and the $2.5 million-the biggest single contribution ever—the company contributed in 1994.

Maybe Amway would have gotten its tax break, and all major legislative fights would turn out exactly the same if the interested parties didn't make campaign contributions. Maybe. But I doubt it. One poll showed 86 percent of Americans believing that campaign contributions influence policy decisions—and that poll was taken before the current scandals. Public perception is important. It affects whether people trust the Congress to do the right thing. And it affects whether people feel it is worth participating in the political system on election day.

Opponents of campaign-finance reform, like Senator Mitch McConnell, Republican of Kentucky, love to wrap themselves in the Constitution. The ACLU is a willing accomplice. The 1976 Supreme Court decision in *Buckley v. Valeo*, which threw out limits on campaign expenditures by candidates, is their battle cry. They argue that every reform proposal aimed at reducing the domination of the political system by big money violates the First Amendment. "Money equals speech," they proclaim. "The First Amendment is not a loophole."

It isn't. But it's not an impenetrable roadblock to reform, either. There is nuance in this area of the law that the ACLU and Senator McConnell prefer to ignore.

The most important thing to remember when the First Amendment is held up like a stop sign against reform is that the *Buckley* decision upheld limits on campaign contributions. Candidates can spend as much as they want on their own campaigns, the Court held, but contributions from citizens should be limited. The Court reasoned that candidates have a right, as a matter of free expression, to spend their own money on their own campaigns. But campaign contributions can create corruption, or the appearance of corruption. So, in the interest of democratic government, they can be curbed. The Court therefore upheld limits on individual contributors of $1,000 per candidate per election. It also upheld a limit of $25,000 on the total annual contributions that individuals may make to candidates, parties, and PACs.

The *Buckley* decision also upheld the system by which we have funded Presidential elections in this country since 1976 with taxpayer money. Simply put, it is constitutional to offer candidates a very tempting inducement—about $60 million in public funds for Presidential candidates in the last election—to limit their spending. The limits in the Presidential system are voluntary. Ross Perot and Steve Forbes decided not to abide by them.

These important components of the *Buckley* decision, which the ACLU argued against at the time and with which it still disagrees, mean that central provisions of the reform bill introduced by Senators John McCain, Republican of Arizona, and Russ Feingold, Democrat of Wisconsin, would be upheld by the Court. Those provisions—a ban on the unlimited corporate, labor union, and individual contributions to the political parties known as "soft money," and voluntary spending limits for Congressional campaigns, made more attractive by the offer of free and reducedrate TV time for those who limit their spending—are worthy and constitutional goals. More far-reaching inducements to candidates to voluntarily limit their spending, like providing clean public money for all Congressional elections, would also pass constitutional muster.

Another difficult but not insurmountable problem is the growing use of phony issue ads to make an end-run around contribution limits and the prohibition on corporate contributions to federal elections. Most of the money the political parties raise goes to pay for TV ads. Television is the single greatest expense for most candidates. Candidates are often happy when their contributors channel money into "issue ads."

Thus we've seen the rise of ads that claim to be about important issues, but actually are thinly veiled campaign advertisements. In 1996, one ad accused a candidate of beating his wife. The ad didn't urge viewers to vote against the candidate, just to call him and "tell him we don't approve of his wrongful behavior." Citizens For Reform, the tax-exempt group founded by conservative activist Peter Flaherty that paid for the ad, spent $2 million in the two months before the election to air ads in fifteen Congressional districts. Triad Management, a Washington, D.C.-based political consulting firm run by a former fund-raiser for Oliver North, helped steer wealthy donors to the group. At least one made a $100,000 contribution.

> *Most of the money the political parties raise goes to pay for TV ads.*

Candidates pay for such ads out of funds that are subject to the election laws; outside groups should, too. *Buckley* itself permits the regulation of ads that expressly advocate the election or defeat of candidates. And in a 1990 decision, *Austin v. Chamber of Commerce*, the Supreme Court recognized the power of the legislature to address "the corrosive and distorting effects of immense aggregations of wealth that are accumulated with the help of the corporate form and that have little or no correlation to the public's support for the corporation's political ideas."

Congress should try to fine-tune the definition of "express advocacy," based on the real-life experience of the 1996 elections. Phony issue ads paid for by corporate funds should not dominate and distort the electoral debate.

Court decisions and FEC rulings, combined with the ingenuity of candidates and outside groups, have shredded the campaign-finance system passed by Congress in the wake of the Watergate scandal. By 1996, we had unlimited campaign spending and unlimited contributions again—only this time through the soft-money and phony issue-ad loophole. And we had more scandals.

How do conservatives respond? By promoting a bill that would make the problem of money in politics even worse. Aptly named for its chief House sponsor, Representative John Doolittle, Republican of California, the bill would wipe out all limits on individual campaign contributions to candidates, PACs, and parties, while requiring all contributions to be disclosed on the Internet within twenty-four hours. The Cato Institute loves this idea: Adam Smith meets the FEC.

A system of unlimited contributions to candidates is frightening to contemplate. Major legislative battles already are cash cows for members of Congress. Under the Doolittle bill, they will be gold mines. Just get on the right committee, open your bank account, and watch the money stream in. The incentive for corporations to launder contributions through employees will be hard to resist and even harder to police. Why raise eyebrows by having twenty-five employees, including some secretaries and clerks, send in $1,000 checks? Just funnel the $25,000 or even $100,000 to your favorite Senator through a wealthy executive.

But won't disclosure solve all these problems? Here's the theory: Just give the public all the information, and if it thinks candidates are for sale to the wrong people, it won't elect them. Sounds good, but it won't work. We actually have a pretty good system of disclosure now. It's not instantaneous, but the information is available fairly quickly, especially in the final month of the campaign. The problem is not disclosure but public access, public understanding, and timing. Not everyone has a computer. Not everyone with a computer has access to the Internet, or the technical capability to obtain campaign-finance information and make sense of it.

Once very rich people can give unlimited amounts directly to candidates or PACs, voters will have an incredible burden added to their decision-making process. And not much information to go on. Even if a vigilant press does its best to help, it won't be enough. The information may also come too late. Political contributions flow throughout the election cycle, as legislation is being considered in Congress. For example, AT&T's PAC distributed $166,000 to federal candidates on a single day in late 1995, the day after a compromise on the telecommunications legislation was reached.

Imagine this scenario: The Doolittle bill is law. Early next year, an electric-utility executive gives $100,000 to the chairman of the Senate Energy Committee, which is marking up the electricity deregulation bill the next week. The Senator, who was reelected in 1996, drops a provision from the bill that would have prohibited utilities from passing on to consumers all of the costs from their failed nuclear plants. A year later, reeling from your swollen electricity bill, you get on your computer and trace the money, figure out the timing of the contribution and the legislation, and decide to act. Congratulations! You can vote against your Senator in 2002.

Campaign Finance Reform: Faulty Assumptions and Undemocratic Consequences[4]

By Bradley A. Smith
USA Today, January 1998

The agenda of the campaign finance reform movement has been to lower the cost of campaigning, reduce the influence of special interests, and open up the political system to change. In 1974, reformers gained their greatest victory, passing major amendments to the Federal Elections Campaign Act. Nevertheless, by 1996, Congressional campaign spending, in constant dollars, nearly had tripled.

Congressional election contributions by political action committees (PACs) increased from $20,500,000 in 1976 to $189,000,000 in 1994. Since 1974, the number of PACs has risen from 608 to more than 4,500. House incumbents outspent challengers in 1996 by almost four to one. Meanwhile, incumbent reelection rates in the House reached record highs in 1986 and 1988, before declining slightly in the 1990s. What went wrong?

The problem is that reform has been based on faulty assumptions and is, in fact, irretrievably undemocratic. Reform proposals inherently favor certain political elites, support the status quo, and discourage grassroots political activity.

FAULTY ASSUMPTIONS

Too much money is spent on campaigns.

The language in which political campaigns are described in the press reinforces the perception that too much money is spent on them. Candidates "amass war chests" with the help of "special interests" which "pour their millions" into campaigns. "Obscene" expenditures "career" out of control or "skyrocket" upwards. Yet, to say that too much money is spent on campaigning is to beg the question, "compared to what?" For instance, Americans expend two to three times as much money each year on potato chips as on political campaigns.

---

4. Article by Bradley A. Smith from *USA Today* January 1998. Copyright © *USA Today*. Reprinted with permission.

In the two-year period ending in November, 1996, approximately $800,000,000 was spent by all Congressional general election candidates. Although this set a record for Congressional races, it amounts to about $4 per eligible voter, spent over a two-year period. Total direct campaign outlays for all candidates for local, state, and Federal elections over the same period can be estimated around $2,500,000,000, or about $12 per eligible voter over the two-year cycle. By comparison, Procter & Gamble and Philip Morris, the nation's two largest advertisers, budget roughly the same amount on advertising as is laid out by all political candidates and parties.

In many cases, those candidates who best are able to raise campaign dollars in small contributions are those who are most emphatically out of the mainstream.

Increased campaign spending does translate into a better informed electorate, and voter understanding of issues grows with the quantity of campaign information received. Candidate ads are the major source of voter information. Lower campaign spending will result in less public awareness and understanding of issues. Considering the importance of elections to any democratic society, it is hard to believe that direct expenditures of approximately $10 per voter for all local, state, and national campaigns over a two-year period is a crisis requiring government regulation and limitations on spending.

Campaigns based on small contributions are more democratic.

As many as 18,000,000 Americans make some financial contribution to a political party, candidate, or PAC in an election cycle. No other system of campaign funding anywhere in the world enjoys so broad a base of support. Yet, this amounts to just 10% of the voting-age population. Even though this figure represents a far broader base of contributors than historically has existed, it has not made the political system more democratic and responsive.

In many cases, those candidates who best are able to raise campaign dollars in small contributions are those who are most emphatically out of the mainstream. Republican Barry Goldwater's 1964 presidential campaign, for example, garnered $5,800,000 from 410,000 small contributors before he suffered a landslide defeat. On his way to an even more crushing defeat in 1972, Democrat George McGovern raised almost $15,000,000 from small donors, at an average of approximately $20 per contributor.

Assuming that reliance on numerous small contributions makes a campaign in some way more democratic, the most "democratic" campaign of recent years was the 1994 Senate race of Republican Oliver North. He amassed approximately $20,000,000, almost entirely from small contributors, and outspent his nearest rival by nearly four-to-one. Yet, he lost to an unpopular opponent plagued by personal scandal.

With the exception of the occasional candidate such as McGovern or North, Americans are unwilling, individually, to contribute enough money in small amounts to run modern campaigns. The likelihood that what any individual does will matter simply is too small to provide most voters with the incentive to give financially to candidates. If large contributions were banned totally, there would not be enough money available to finance campaigns at a level that informs the electorate.

Money buys elections.

A candidate with little or no money to spend is unlikely to win most races. Furthermore, the one expending the most wins more often than not. The correlation between spending and victory, though, may stem simply from the desire of donors to contribute to candidates who are likely to win, in which case the ability to win attracts money, rather than the other way around. Similarly, higher levels of campaign contributions to a candidate may reflect a level of public support that is manifested later at the polls.

A greater outlay does not necessarily translate into electoral triumph. Having money means having the ability to be heard; it does not mean that voters will like what they hear. In 1994 House of Representative races, for example, 34 Republicans defeated Democratic incumbents, spending on average two-thirds as much as their opponents. In 1996, several Senate candidates won despite being outspent. Republican Michael Huffington spent nearly $30,000,000 of his own money in the 1994 California senatorial race, only to come up empty-handed.

Money is a corrupting influence on the legislature.

A substantial majority of those who have studied voting patterns on a systemic basis agree that campaign contributions affect very few votes in the legislature. The primary factors in determining a legislator's votes are party affiliation, ideology, and constituent views and needs. Where contributions and voting patterns intersect, this is largely because donors contribute to candidates believed to favor their positions, not the other way around.

These empirical studies often cut against intuition. Experience and human nature suggest that people are influenced by money, even when it does not go directly into their pockets, but into their campaigns. Yet, there are good reasons why the impact of contributions is not so great. First, people who are attracted to public office generally have strong personal views on issues. Second, there are institutional and political incentives to support party positions. Third, large contributors usually are offset in legislative debate by equally well-financed interests that contribute to a different group of candidates. Large PACs and organizations frequently suffer enormous losses in the legislative process.

Moreover, money is not the only political commodity of value. For instance, the National Rifle Association has a large PAC, but also has nearly 3,000,000 members who focus intently, even solely, on NRA issues in their voting. The NRA's power would seem to come less from dollars than from votes. To the extent that it comes from dollars, that, too, is a function of votes—i.e., the group's large membership. Groups advocating gun control frequently complain that the NRA outspends them, but rarely mention that the NRA outvotes them as well.

Campaign finance reformers often pose as disinterested citizens, merely seeking "good government." In fact, there is ample evidence that they have targeted certain types of campaign activities closely tied to political agendas reformers oppose. They therefore favor regulation that would tilt the electoral process in favor of preferred candidates, against popular will.

NEGATIVE CONSEQUENCES

Campaign finance reform has had several negative consequences, which broadly can be labeled "undemocratic." Reform has entrenched the status quo and made the electoral system less responsive to popular opinion, strengthened the power of elites, favored wealthy individuals, and limited opportunities for "grassroots" political activity.

Entrenching the status quo.

Contribution limits favor incumbents by making it relatively harder for challengers to raise money to run their campaigns. The need to solicit cash from a large number of small contributors benefits incumbent candidates who have in place a database of past givers, an intact campaign organization, and the ability to raise funds on an ongoing basis from political action committees.

Newcomers with low name recognition have the most difficulty raising substantial sums from small contributors, who are less likely to give to unknowns. Well-known public figures challenging the status quo traditionally have relied on a small number of wealthy patrons to fund their campaigns. Theodore Roosevelt's 1912 Bull Moose campaign was funded almost entirely by a handful of wealthy supporters. Eugene McCarthy's 1968 anti-war campaign relied for seed money on a handful of six-figure donors, including industrialist Stewart Mott, who gave approximately $210,000, and Wall Street banker Jack Dreyfus, Jr., who may have contributed as much as $500,000.

More recently, John Anderson probably would have had more success in his independent campaign for the presidency in 1980 had his wealthy patron, Mott, been able to give unlimited amounts to his campaign. Whereas Ross Perot's 1992 presidential campaign was made possible by the Supreme Court's holding that an individual may spend unlimited sums to advance his own candidacy, contribution limits make it illegal for Perot to bankroll the campaign of another challenger, such as Colin Powell, in the same manner. The Reform Party, started in 1996, was able to get off the ground, in large part, thanks to Perot's money.

Beyond making it harder for challengers to raise cash, contribution limits indirectly reduce spending. This further works against challengers. Incumbents begin each election with significant advantages in name recognition. They are able to attract press coverage because of their office and often receive assistance from their office staffs and government-paid constituent mailings. Through patronage and constituent favors, they can add to their support.

To offset these advantages, challengers must expend money. Studies have found that the effect of each dollar spent is much greater for challengers than for incumbents because most voters already have some knowledge about incumbents and their records. Since spending is so much more important for challengers than incumbents, lower limits tend to hurt the former more.

Set low enough, contribution and spending limits make it almost impossible for challengers to attain the critical threshold of name recognition at which point a race becomes competitive. The bills introduced unsuccessfully in the last two Congresses by Senators John McCain (R.-Ariz.) and Russell Feingold (D.-Wis.) included spending limits. In 1994 and 1996, every challenger who spent less than the limits in the McCain-Feingold bill lost, but each incumbent who expended less than the proposed limits won.

Influence peddling and accountability.

Like all political activity, the purpose of campaign contributions is to influence public policy. Contributors may adopt a legislative strategy, attempting to influence votes in the legislature, or an electoral strategy, aimed at influencing who wins elections. Influence peddling only becomes a problem when legislative strategies are pursued; under an electoral strategy, groups are trying to persuade the public to vote for a preferred candidate, and there is nothing wrong with that. Yet, contribution limits—the most popular reform measure—encourage legislative strategies by PACs and other monied interests.

> *Newcomers with low name recognition have the most difficulty raising substantial sums from small contributors, who are less likely to give to unknowns.*

Campaign contributors must weigh the costs and benefits of each strategy. Normally, they prefer an electoral strategy, aimed at convincing voters to elect like-minded candidates to office. Money given to a losing challenger is not merely a waste, it can be counterproductive, since such contributions increase the enmity of the incumbent. Because incumbents win most races, an electoral strategy of supporting challengers is a very high risk.

The alternative is to give to the incumbent in the hope that a legislative strategy might succeed, at least by minimizing otherwise hostile treatment aimed at the contributor's interests. When contributions are limited to an amount unlikely to change the result of an election, rational donors are forced into a legislative strategy. Thus, to the extent that campaign contributions influence legislative policymaking, limits are likely to make the situation worse.

Furthermore, PACs—and the interests they represent—play an important role in monitoring an office-holder's record. In most cases, it will not be rational for individuals to devote considerable time to monitoring the performance of elected officials, but, by banding together with others having similar concerns, they can perform that function at a reasonable cost. PACs are an important part of this process. Thus, contribution limits may reduce legislative monitoring, leading to a legislature ever more isolated from the people.

Favoring select elites.

Campaign finance reform usually is sold as a populist means to strengthen the power of "ordinary" citizens against "big money" interests. In fact, campaign finance reform has favored select elites and further isolated individuals from the political process.

There are a great many sources of political influence. Hollywood personalities, by virtue of their celebrity, may receive an audience for their political views they would not have otherwise. They may be invited to testify before Congress, despite their lack of any particular expertise, or use their celebrity to assist campaigns through appearances at rallies. Successful academics may write powerful articles that change the way people think about issues. Labor organizers have at their disposal a vast supply of manpower that can be used to support favored candidates. Successful entrepreneurs may amass large sums of money, which can be applied for political purposes. Media editors, reporters, and anchors can shape not only the manner in which news is reported, but what is reported. Those with marketing skills can raise funds or produce advertising for a candidate or cause.

> *Media editors, reporters, and anchors can shape not only the manner in which news is reported, but what is reported.*

Newspapers, magazines, and TV and radio stations can spend unlimited sums to promote the election of favored candidates. Thus, Katherine Graham, the publisher of the *Washington Post,* has at her disposal the resources of a media empire to promote her views, free from the campaign finance restrictions others are subjected to. News anchor Peter Jennings is given a nightly forum on national TV on which to express his opinions.

Media elites are not the sole group whose influence is heightened by campaign spending and contribution limits. Restricting the flow of money into campaigns increases the relative importance of in-kind contributions, and so favors those who are able to control large blocks of manpower, rather than dollars. Limiting contributions and expenditures does not particularly democratize the process, but merely shifts power from people who give money to those whose primary contribution is time, media access, or some other attribute—i.e., from small business groups to labor unions and journalists. Other beneficiaries of campaign finance limitations include political middlemen; public relations firms conducting "voter education" programs; lobbyists; PACs, such as Emily's List, which "bundle" large numbers of $1,000 contributions; and political activists. These individuals probably are less representative of public opinion than the wealthy philanthropists and industrialists who financed campaigns in the past.

Campaign finance restrictions do not make the system more responsive to the interests of the middle and working class. Efforts to assure equality of inputs into the campaign process are less likely to guarantee popular control than is the presence of multiple sources of political power. Campaign finance regulation reduces the number of voices and increases the power of those groups whose form of contribution remains unregulated.

Favoring wealthy candidates.

Though campaign finance restrictions aim to reduce the role of money in politics, they have helped to renew the phenomenon of the "millionaire candidate," of whom Huffington and Perot arguably are the most celebrated examples. The Supreme Court has held that Congress may not limit constitutionally the amount a candidate can spend on his or her own campaign. Access to unlimited amounts, coupled with restrictions on raising money, favors those candidates who can contribute large sums to their own campaigns from personal assets. A Michael Huffington, Herb Kohl, or Jay Rockefeller becomes a particularly attractive candidate precisely because personal wealth provides a direct campaign advantage that can not be offset by a large contributor to the opposing candidate.

At the same time that contribution limits help wealthy candidates, they tend to harm working-class political interests. A candidate with many supporters who can afford to give the legal limit may be relatively unscathed by "reform" legislation. However, candidates with large constituencies among the poor and working class traditionally have obtained their campaign funds from a small base of wealthy donors. By limiting the ability of wealthy individuals such as Stewart Mott or Augustus Belmont to finance these efforts, working-class constituencies may suffer.

FAVORING SPECIAL INTERESTS

Campaign finance regulation also is undemocratic in that it favors well-organized special interests over grassroots political activity. Limitations on campaign contributions and spending require significant regulation of the campaign process. They favor those already familiar with the regulatory machinery and people with the money and sophistication to hire the lawyers, accountants, and lobbyists needed to comply with complex filing requirements. Such dynamics naturally will run against newcomers to the political arena, especially those who are less educated or less able to pay for professional services.

As opportunities to gain an advantage over an opponent through use of the regulatory process are created, litigation has become a major campaign tactic. One can expect such tactics to be used most often by those already familiar with the rules, and there is some evidence that campaign enforcement actions are directed disproportionately at challengers, who are less likely to have staff familiar with the intricacies of campaign finance regulation.

Perhaps those most likely to run afoul of campaign finance laws—and thus to be vulnerable to legal manipulations aimed at driving them from the political debate—are those engaged in true grassroots activities. For instance, in 1991, the *Los Angeles Times* reviewed Federal Election Commission files and found that one of the largest groups of campaign law violators consisted of "elderly persons . . . with little grasp of the federal campaign laws."

Even sophisticated interest groups have found campaign finance laws a substantial hindrance to grassroots campaign activity and voter education efforts. In 1994, the U.S. Chamber of Commerce and American Medical Association decided not to publish and distribute candidate endorsements to thousands of their dues-paying members, under threats of litigation from the Federal Election Commission. Under FEC regulations, just 63 of the Chamber of Commerce's 220,000 dues-paying members qualified as "members" for the purposes of receiving the organization's political communications. Similarly, the FEC had held that it would be unlawful for the AMA to distribute endorsements to about 44,500 of its members.

The First Amendment was based on the belief that political speech was too important to be regulated by the government. Campaign finance laws operate on the directly contrary assumption that campaigns are so important that speech must be regulated. Campaign finance laws constitute an arcane web of regulation that has led to citizens being fined for distributing homemade leaflets and trade groups being prohibited from communicating with their members.

The solution to the campaign finance dilemma is to recognize the flawed assumptions of the campaign finance reformers, dismantle the Federal Elections Campaign Act and the FEC bureaucracy, and take seriously the system of campaign finance "regulation" that the Founding Fathers wrote into the Bill of Rights: "Congress shall make no law . . . abridging the freedom of speech."

Campaign Primer's First Lesson:
Cash Flows from Contacts[5]

By Guy Gugliotta
Washington Post, May 18, 1997

The first thing Bob Torricelli did when he decided to run for Congress was write down the names of everyone he had ever known. His mother was first, followed by his father. Beside each name he wrote "$1,000."

Next came friends from the neighborhood, for "considerably less," Torricelli said, but he pressed on. "It took hours," he remembered, but as a young political operative he knew that money and the ability to raise it were critical prerequisites in modern campaigning. Today, freshman Sen. Robert G. Torricelli (D-N.J.), elected in 1996 after 14 years in the House, is a recognized master who lectures on fund-raising to would-be candidates at the Democratic Senatorial Campaign Committee, where he is vice chairman.

In response to a request from *The Washington Post,* he agreed to describe in detail his techniques and how they served him in his 1996 Senate campaign against Rep. Dick Zimmer (R-N.J.). Zimmer declined a similar request.

What Torricelli provided was a look inside modern campaign finance and a primer on how one politician used a life's worth of friendships, political alliances, policy positions, votes and ideological biases to raise millions. "You are building a corporation in a matter of months," he said. "And you are testing it on a single day."

He had contacts in the defense industry, in an Indianapolis insurance company, in a New Orleans oil company and in the office of the Virgin Islands governor. "All I ask is that you open your home, have some friends or associates in, and I'll do the rest," Torricelli said.

Torricelli raised $399,000 in South Florida, mostly among Cuban American supporters of anti-Castro policies he developed. He also raised money from Portuguese Americans, Greek Americans, Chinese Americans, Pakistani Americans and Iranian Americans.

---

5. Article by Guy Gugliotta from the *Washington Post* May 18, 1997. Copyright © *Washington Post.* Reprinted with permission.

Torricelli attended more than 300 fund-raisers in a campaign that began in August 1995, and spent three hours on the telephone every day asking for money. The goal was to spend $1 for every $20 raised.

Polls show that most voters distrust politicians and the money that supports them, and Torricelli agrees with many of his congressional colleagues that the system "collapsed" in 1996, succumbing to millions of dollars in unregulated party "soft money" and special interest expenditures.

Campaign finance abuse and excess have triggered multiple inquiries into the Clinton administration's fund-raising methods. Campaign funding also lies at the heart of Republican House Speaker Newt Gingrich's ethical difficulties.

While few of the questionable practices may involve crimes, the scandals of 1996 have enhanced the appearance of corruption in the system and prompted lawmakers to introduce several reform proposals: set spending limits, abolish soft money and limit interest group participation in campaigns.

None of these proposals is advancing as each party tries to protect its stake in the status quo. In this ambience, Torricelli is a realist who makes no apologies for his expertise in navigating the system. In fact, he asserts that the ability to dive into the swamp and survive is almost a rite of political passage. "We make hard decisions in Congress," Torricelli said. "I'd like to know that everybody walked through fire to get here."

Torricelli defeated Zimmer 1,519,328 votes to 1,227,817. Torricelli estimates about $12.5 million was spent on his behalf, including $9.2 million he raised personally. Zimmer personally raised $8.2 million, Federal Election Commission records show, but with a helping hand from the national GOP, Torricelli said, the money race ended in a virtual dead heat.

For Susan Torricelli, the senator's chief fund-raiser and former wife, 1996 was an election year no different than any other, dictated by the need to raise television money. Yes, she said, "there's more scrutiny" after the fact, but "I'm not saying that people were doing things wrong."

Within the rules, however, political pros regard the Torricelli-Zimmer campaign as a prime example of a crumbling system. Interest groups and political parties poured cash into a race denounced from its beginning for its lack of substance, its focus on money, its reliance on misleading, negative television ads and its vicious—and largely unfounded—personal attacks.

Zimmer accused Torricelli of mob connections and associating with an international fugitive. Torricelli accused Zimmer of taking mob money, voting for ocean dumping and lying about receiving gun lobby contributions.

Through it all, however, Torricelli's fund-raising machine purred among dozens of small networks of supporters, from Jersey chiropractors to high-rollers from Vegas, from his home base in Englewood, N.J., to the movie studios of Beverly Hills.

FEC records show Torricelli raised 61 percent of his money in New Jersey, while Zimmer raised 71 percent. The nonpartisan Center for Responsive Politics said Torricelli raised $992,903 from political action committees (PACs), with the biggest piece ($403,000) coming from organized labor, a typical pattern for Democrats.

Zimmer raised $1.3 million from PACs, the center said, the vast majority from business or professional organizations ($1.1 million), typical for Republicans. Also typical: nearly 80 PACs gave to both candidates.

Torricelli gave back a $1,000 contribution from Democratic fund-raiser John Huang, the target of several federal investigations, and received about 30 contributions from people who had coffee at the White House. Zimmer received nine contributions from members of the Clinton administration's coffee list.

In one apparent departure from convention, pro-Israel PACs favored Torricelli $28,000 to $19,000 for Zimmer, who is Jewish. "To tell you the truth, I didn't know who Dick Zimmer was," said Denver attorney Norman Brownstein, a vice president of the American Israel Public Affairs Committee. But Torricelli, he said, was a longtime supporter of Israel and a highly visible member of the House International Relations Committee, once known as the Foreign Affairs Committee. Last April Brownstein raised almost $6,000 for Torricelli at a Denver breakfast.

"A lot of [House] members duck Foreign Affairs because it doesn't bring lots of money to your district," Torricelli noted. "But I never felt disadvantaged." In raising money in ethnic communities, he added, "nobody does it better than me."

"He was always accessible to us," agreed Paramus, N.J., accountant Andy Comodromos, who remembers the time Torricelli took some Greek American constituents to Cyprus in the early 1980s. When Torricelli ran for the Senate, Comodromos helped translate the district's biennial Greek American fund-raiser into a $25,000 statewide gala with then-presidential adviser George Stephanopoulos as the featured speaker.

Torricelli, 45, is a political risk-taker with a pro-labor voting record and tough stands on gun control and human rights. But he bucked his party in supporting the Persian Gulf War and in drafting the 1992 Cuban Democracy Act, tightening sanctions on the Castro government.

He got his political start as a young attorney working for then-New Jersey Gov. Brendan T. Byrne (D) in the 1970s, then joined the administration of President Jimmy Carter, where he served as an assistant to Vice President Walter F. Mondale.

Torricelli stayed with Mondale after the 1980 elections, until, at the end of 1981, "I decided it was my time." Late one night after dinner with Mondale in a Tokyo hotel, he returned to his room, picked up a yellow legal pad and began to scribble the names "of every person I had known in my life—and a number." The list has been with Torricelli ever since.

During his House career, Torricelli established contact with county Democratic Party officials across New Jersey, he said, and he moved quickly to enter the Senate race when Sen. Bill Bradley (D-N.J.) announced his retirement in August 1995.

"We figured it would take $6 million, spending 85 to 90 percent of it on television," Torricelli said. At that moment, he had a $1.3 million war chest, already a hefty lead over fellow House incumbent Zimmer, who had a bit over $631,000.

New Jersey is the nation's most urban state, and free network television reaches every corner. The catch, as both parties know, is that New Jersey has no network market of its own, so statewide candidates must buy their TV time in New York, the country's most expensive market, and Philadelphia, the fifth most expensive.

Candidates need millions to compete, but under federal election law, individual donors can give only $1,000 to a candidate for the primary and the general election, while PACs can give $5,000 in each cycle. This "hard money" is the mother's milk of American politics, but politicians readily admit that raising it a tiny nugget at a time is pure drudgery.

But Torricelli was good at it. In late 1995 an old friend from the insurance business raised about $10,000 for him among company employees in Indianapolis. In Las Vegas, friends in the gambling industry raised nearly $30,000.

The Coleman family of New Jersey sponsored an event at their New Orleans oil company affiliate that earned around $12,000. Ken Pincourt, an executive Torricelli met through House Minority Leader Richard A. Gephardt (D-Mo.), raised nearly $40,000 at a Palm Beach, Fla., event. Virgin Islands Gov. Richard L. Schneider, whose Washington representative met Torricelli at a Young Democrats convention in 1975, arranged a St. Croix event that raised $20,000.

In March, New Jersey Council of Chiropractors President Gerald Mattia, who met Torricelli during the 1994 health care debate, invited 3,000 colleagues to contribute, raising almost $15,000. "Chiropractors talk to more people in a day than anybody else in New Jersey," Torricelli said.

In December 1995, Torricelli raised more than $65,000 at a Miami fund-raiser sponsored by Cuban Americans. He returned to South Florida repeatedly for nearly a year, making more than in any states except New Jersey and New York.

"If you have a good cause, raising money is simple, and the freedom of Cuba is a wonderful cause," said Miami nurseryman and anti-Castro activist Tony Costa, who hosted a Torricelli fund-raiser. "We are very appreciative of those who help us."

It wasn't all smooth as silk, however. In March 1996, Ruth Dugan, who had known Torricelli since the Byrne years, co-hosted a $2,000-per-person Saddle River, N.J., fund-raiser with Donna Walsh at a mansion owned by Donna's husband, Frank, a trucking executive.

It turned out that Frank, a client of Ruth's attorney husband, Jim, had gone to prison in the 1980s for paying bribes to a mob-influenced union. "In retrospect it wasn't a good idea," Jim Dugan said of the March event. Zimmer used the fund-raiser to imply a Torricelli link to organized crime.

Despite this glitch, June 30, 1996, FEC reports showed Torricelli with $6 million in the bank to Zimmer's $2.5 million, and Torricelli thought victory was at hand. But at that point, he said, the national Republican Party began to spend large amounts of unregulated soft money.

Parties spend soft money on "issue advocacy" ads that do not specifically call for the election or defeat of a candidate and are difficult to document. Torricelli and the Republicans agreed that the Democrats spent $1.3 million on his behalf, but GOP sources could not confirm Torricelli's contention that Republicans spent $4 million for Zimmer.

Still, Torricelli said he felt he had been ambushed, and did "what I swore I would never do," try to match GOP soft money with his own hard dollars, usually a quick way to go bankrupt and lose.

Two trips to Miami yielded around $35,000. On Sept. 26 New Jersey contributors gave him about $29,000. Four days later he raised almost $6,000 at breakfast in Providence, R.I., with Ed Maggiacomo, an old party boss that Torricelli knew from Mondale days.

In late October, Frank Biondi, an MCA entertainment executive Torricelli met through Italian American groups, organized a Beverly Hills luncheon that produced at least $35,000. Torricelli flew to Los Angeles overnight, spent 2 1/2 hours at the event and returned to New Jersey the same evening.

Torricelli believes he was able to win because he hung in against Zimmer's soft money.

With the system in tatters and little prospect for meaningful campaign reform, Torricelli said, candidates can expect more surprises in 1998. "If you campaign on your memory of previous campaigns," he said, "you're at a disadvantage."

AMASSING $25 MILLION

The two candidates in the 1996 New Jersey Senate race spent a combined $25 million, most of that on TV ads. Here is a look at where Dick Zimmer (R) and Robert G. Torricelli (D) got the money.

Torricelli's campaign:

300	Fund-raising events
14,519	Individual donors
8,835	Donors who gave less than $250
$1.35 million	Transferred from House to Senate campaign
$9.1 million	Total amount spent
$7.8 million	Spent on television ads

Total receipts $9.2 million

Spending on issue ads on behalf of candidate:

From party:	$1.3 million from DNC and state committees
From outside groups:	$1 million from Sierra Club, AFL-CIO and Citizen Action
PAC contributions:	$993,000 (10.8% of total)
Out-of-state money:	39%

Outside states with highest contributions:

N.Y.	$899,000
Fla.	$399,000
Calif.	$194,000
Pa.	$149,000

Zimmer: **Total receipts** $8.2 million

Spending on issue ads on behalf of candidate:

From party:	$4 million (Torricelli's estimate) from RNC and state and national committees
From outside groups:	$500,000 from Americans for Tax Reform
PAC contributions:	$1.31 million (14.3% of total)
Out-of-state money:	29%

Outside states with highest contributions:

N.Y.	$537,000
Pa.	156,000

Torricelli's top contributing PAC sectors:

Labor	$403,000
Ideological and single-issue PACs	98,273
Financial, insurance and real estate	75,400
Lawyers and lobbyists	73,000
Health	67,000

Zimmer's top contributing PAC sectors:

Financial, insurance and real estate	$322,195
Miscellaneous business	227,228
Health	157,200
Ideological and single-issue PACs	133,274
Agriculture	101,600

SOURCES: Sen. Robert G. Torricelli, Center for Responsive Politics

Free Money[6]

By James V. DeLong
Reason, August/September 2000

Once again we are preparing to choose federal, state, and local officials to preside over governments that redistribute about 38 percent of the GNP, enact and administer thousands of criminal laws, and assert an open-ended right to regulate every aspect of our lives. And once again the subjects of this power think they should be allowed to influence the outcome. People want to donate money to the candidates they favor, tell potential voters about candidates and issues, expand the channels of information beyond the conventional media, form organizations with others of like mind, establish Internet sites, and, in general, *participate*.

This desire to participate upsets most journalists, many politicians, and a large percentage of the nation's intellectual and financial elites. The Web site of Common Cause (*www.commoncause.org/publications/campaign_finance.htm*), the organization that for 25 years has been the mainspring of the campaign for election finance reform, features alarmist headlines such as "Ka-Ching: National Parties Raise Record $160.5 Million in Soft Money through First 15 Months of 2000 Election Cycle." The Committee for Economic Development (*www.ced.org*), a voice of the business establishment, is equally concerned, blaming the "vast sums of unregulated 'soft money'" for all the ills of the current electoral process and advocating fundamental reforms to "restore trust and balance."

During this year's Republican primaries, John McCain used the campaign finance issue to harvest great media acclaim and boost his candidacy. The topic played poorly with the nonestablishment parts of the Republican Party, both social and economic conservatives. They understood that McCain was telling the party to commit suicide, since his reforms would have disarmed Republican constituencies while leaving the power of labor unions, government employees, and celebrities untouched.

Still, the issue has enough media traction that George W. Bush has made reform noises. He proposes a ban on "soft money" contributions to parties by unions and corporations, along with stronger protections for union members who don't want their dues used for

---

6. Reprinted with permission, from Aug./Sept. 2000 issue of *Reason Magazine*. Copyright © 2000 by the Reason Foundation, 3415 S. Sepulveda Blvd., Suite 400, Los Angeles, CA 90034 *www.reason.com*.

political purposes with which they disagree. These changes would affect Democrats as well as Republicans, so they will never pass. Al Gore, of course, favors reform, as long as he gets to define it. He would eliminate all "soft money" but allow everyone, including unions and corporations, to contribute to a nonpartisan fund that would be used to pay for the campaigns of congressional candidates who agree to spending limits.

As reflected in Gore's plan, critics of the current system tend to focus on the "loopholes" they believe undermine noble but inadequate attempts to control corruption. In particular, they decry "soft money" contributions to political parties, which are not subject to statutory limits, and spending by groups that care deeply about particular issues and want to communicate their

> *Washington may have been the last president not to be subjected to complaints about the evil power of money.*

concerns to candidates and the public. Yet almost everything the reformers say about "loopholes" is flat-out wrong. The practices branded as loopholes are not only legitimate, they are the best part of the system. Every lover of democracy and freedom should be working to expand them until they swallow the absurd rules that currently govern campaign finance. Given the inevitable failure of the Federal Election Commission's dithering efforts to regulate political speech on the Internet, that day may not be far off.

Evil Influence

In the campaign of 1789, George Washington spent [sterling] 39 on "treats" for the voters. This was not much, but he was the only candidate and there weren't many voters. Washington may have been the last president not to be subjected to complaints about the evil power of money. By 1800, when Jefferson beat Adams, the financial power of banks played a role. By the post-Civil War era, both parties were shaking down public employees for contributions; in Pennsylvania during the 1870s, Republicans demanded 2 percent of their salaries. After civil service reform dried up this revenue source, the parties turned to the newest pot of wealth, big corporations.

The election of 1896 is generally cited as the great watershed in campaign finance. Mark Hanna, an Ohio industrialist, raised $7 million ($100 million in today's dollars) to help William McKinley beat William Jennings Bryan. The money came from corporations dedicated to the gold standard and protective tariffs, and Hanna asked them to contribute their "fair share," reflecting their stake in the general prosperity. His approach struck another modern note, says historian Thomas Fleming: "Hanna refused to promise any specific favor or service; rather, he sold the glittering concept of 'access' and a government that smiled on corporations."

Sympathy for Bryan is not entirely in order, because the populist's backers were wealthy individuals, notably financier Augustus Belmont of New York. But Hanna's tactics prompted a public outcry, and after McKinley's assassination in 1901 corporate America got Theodore Roosevelt, who was willing to ride the rising public concern about business money. A $50,000 check from New York Life to Roosevelt's 1904 campaign received unpleasant publicity, so, in another modern touch, he learned from his mistakes and proposed a ban on all political contributions and the funding of campaigns by the government.

Congress did not go that far, but it did ban corporate contributions to federal elections in 1907, require disclosure in 1910, impose expenditure limits in 1911, and require yet more disclosure in 1925. During the New Deal, Republican fears of the new army of bureaucrats brought about the Hatch Act of 1939, which limited government employees' political activity. As a balancer, caps were imposed on individual contributions to campaigns and on expenditures on presidential elections. The rising power of unions was attacked in 1943, when they, like corporations, were forbidden to contribute to federal campaigns.

It did not take long to find loopholes in these reforms. For example, the parties quickly decided that the 1939 limits on contributions and expenditures applied only to individual committees and that there was no limit on the number of committees a party could form. The 1940 election was characterized by multiple committees, no real limits on either contributions or expenditures for anyone who knew enough to write more than one check, and a new record for money spent on a presidential election: $21 million, or $257 million in 2000 dollars.

Costs kept rising—Johnson vs. Goldwater cost $60 million in 1964, Nixon vs. Humphrey $100 million in 1968 ($331 million and $492 million, respectively in current dollars)—and the issue finally erupted in the 1970s. In 1971 Congress passed a mild bill, directed mostly at disclosure. The election of 1972 set new records for spending ($400 million for all parties in all races, or $1.6 billion in current dollars) and was followed by the post-Watergate disclosures of sleazy tactics. With the public aroused, the result was the Federal Election Campaign Act of 1974.

It was promptly challenged by one of the oddest coalitions ever to enter a courtroom. The plaintiffs included conservative New York Sen. James Buckley (brother of William F.), liberal Sen. Eugene

McCarthy, the American Civil Liberties Union, the Mississippi Republican Party, and the Libertarian Party. In *Buckley v. Valeo,* the U.S. Supreme Court rightly found that large chunks of the law violated the First Amendment right of free speech. Other provisions were upheld, though, based on distinctions not readily apparent to the naked eye.

Buckley was quickly followed by important decisions of the new Federal Election Commission (which had been established by the

---

Free speech rights are not easily reconciled with the laws passed in the 1970s.

1974 law) and then by more congressional action in response to both the Court and the FEC. When the dust settled, we had pretty much our current system, though there have been some tweaks since, largely in the form of FEC and judicial interpretations of the '74 law.

Speech Impediments

The fundamental problem with controlling campaign finance involves free speech. How can government constitutionally prohibit someone, whether an individual or a corporation, from running an ad that says "Candidate X is a schmuck" or "Candidate Y voted for higher defense budgets?" In fact, given First Amendment precedents, how can the government prevent a citizen from donating money for a candidate to spend on such messages? Free speech rights are not easily reconciled with the laws passed in the 1970s, and the courts have spent a quarter-century in the delicate political task of accommodating reformist alarms without doing excessive violence to the Constitution.

The task is complicated by the reality that campaign laws present a stark fox-guarding-the-henhouse scenario: Except for judicial enforcement of the Constitution, incumbents have carte blanche to write the rules under which people will try to unseat them. Any legislators who cannot protect themselves forever are too dumb to deserve to stay in office. In 1998, political action committees gave $220 million to congressional races; 78 percent went to incumbents, 10 percent to challengers, and 12 percent to candidates in open-seat races.

The courts are not big on contemporary political theory, and they rarely make use of public choice models that assume politicians, like actors in the private sector, relentlessly seek to increase their market share. The models of administrative law the courts do use are all based on treacly New Deal platitudes. Nonetheless, many judges, especially in the U.S. circuit courts, are aware of the campaign laws' potential as incumbent-protection devices, and this awareness infuses their decisions, however subtly. In *Shrink Missouri Government v. Adams* (1998), for example, the U.S. Court of Appeals for the 8th Circuit expressed skepticism about the testimony of various state legislators concerning the need to battle "corruption," noting that they had failed to cite any actual instances.

In *Buckley*, the Supreme Court struck down provisions of the 1974 law imposing limits on expenditures in House and Senate races. It also threw out, as an unconstitutional abridgement of free speech, limits on how much a wealthy person can spend on his own campaign. But limits on how much a person can give to someone else's campaign were upheld, and so were limits on how much an individual can give to all campaigns in a single year. Money, in the Court's view, somehow loses its character as speech when it leaves the donor's hands. Stewart Mott, the heir to a fortune in General Motors stock who largely funded Eugene McCarthy's 1968 insurgency, would no longer be able to do such a thing, though he could run himself and spend as much as he wanted. Hence the candidacy of Steve Forbes, who had to carry the economic reform banner himself because he was not allowed to finance a campaign by anyone else.

The contribution limits—$1,000 to individual campaigns and $5,000 to PACs per year, up to a total of $25,000 per year—have not been raised since 1974, even though inflation has reduced their real value by two-thirds. The next time some incumbent moans about how much time he spends raising money, think of how simple it would be to increase the limits, and suppress your sympathy. The limits may make an incumbent's life unpleasant, but they make a challenger's impossible, and that is why they remain.

Pre-1974 bans on campaign contributions by corporations and unions remained in place, except that the 1974 law allows these organizations to pay the costs of administering political action committees. PACs can collect contributions from individuals and dole them out to candidates, subject to the limit on the amount contributed to any single campaign.

The law also established the FEC to administer the system, write regulations, and implement myriad reporting requirements imposed on everyone who dabbles in elections. This has led to a numbing array of nit-picking rules. The FEC's *Campaign Guide for Corporations and Labor Unions* is 80 pages long, and the print is small. There are separate guides for party committees, for candidates, and for PACs. The FEC digest of court cases on the law decided between 1976 and September 1999 contains 328 entries. The list of FEC advisory opinions issued since 1977 totals more than 1,130. These concern issues such as whether companies may reimburse their employees for making campaign contributions (forbidden) and whether fathers may funnel dollars through their kids (also forbidden, but you can use your spouse, as long as both names are on the account and both sign the check).

Forbidden Words

The biggest regulatory challenges come from those areas that reformers call "loopholes" and others call the exercise of free speech rights. These fall into three categories: independent expenditures, soft money, and volunteer activity.

An independent expenditure is spending by someone outside a campaign that is not coordinated with the campaign. Advertising is the most obvious example, but the category also encompasses material such as voter guides. If these were classified as campaign contributions, it would be illegal for businesses, unions, and non-profit corporations to make them at all. For individuals, their cost would count against contribution limits.

In 1974, Congress, acting just as a public choice theorist would predict, did indeed try to control independent expenditures. But the pesky Supreme Court would not agree. In *Buckley*, it read the statute narrowly so as to avoid constitutional problems (a tried and true legal technique), saying the prohibition of corporate expenditures "in connection with an election" extended only to contributions to candidates and "express advocacy," which meant ads using phrases like "Vote for Candidate X" or "Defeat Candidate Y."

"Issue ads" that present an argument and perhaps link it to a candidate but that stop short of express advocacy are not covered by the law. Similarly, other expenditures of all sorts are allowed as long as they are not coordinated with a particular campaign. A later case held that even express advocacy is protected if it is conducted by a nonprofit corporation and is not coordinated with a candidate's campaign. (*A fortiori*, this applies to individuals.) The FEC has moved to bring such spending into the system, though, counting donations to advocacy groups against limits on individual contributions to candidates and requiring extensive reporting.

After *Buckley*, groups with a stake in elections learned the arts of independent action and issue advocacy. Unions poured $40 million into the 1996 election, environmentalists use issue advocacy regularly, and various conservative groups depend on it. To reformers, this participation by groups that care about issues is a "loophole."

A brisk legal business advises people how to walk the line between issue advocacy, which escapes regulation, and express advocacy. To the FEC, an ad saying, "Higher defense spending is good; Congressman X is opposed to it," is express advocacy. But if it says, "Higher defense spending is good; write Congressman X and tell him to change his position," it is an issue ad. The FEC keeps pushing to expand the law's coverage, and the courts, for the most part, keep pushing back.

In one of the weirder aspects of this odd field, the definition of express advocacy differs in the East and the West. The U.S. Court of Appeals for the 9th Circuit, which covers California and eight other states, supports a squishy FEC test that says it all depends on what you intended to do. Other circuits say that only the precise words mentioned in *Buckley* and their synonyms are covered.

Lifeblood of the Party

The second big alleged loophole is called "soft money." State and national political parties are allowed to collect funds for general "party building" activities without having these count against the donors' annual contribution limits. Perhaps more important, these contributions can come from unions and corporations, entities that cannot give directly to campaigns at all. The parties must report the money to the FEC, and they must not coordinate their spending with campaigns.

The current deluge of soft money stems from a 1978 FEC advisory opinion that expanded the extent to which the parties could use such funds for purposes such as registration and get-out-the-vote drives. Predictably, these activities are now given an expansive reading, encompassing major electioneering. In 1992, the major parties collected $86 million in soft money, but its utility was still thought to be limited because everyone assumed that if they tried to push much beyond registration and get-out-the-vote drives, they would cross the line into illegal coordination. The FEC took the view that party committees were too close to the candidates to be independent and thus could never meet the requirement that expenditures on advertising or materials not be coordinated with a campaign.

Two things happened in 1996 to change this. The Supreme Court decided that a Republican state committee in Colorado that ran ads against a Democratic senatorial candidate was in fact independent of the Republican candidate. More important, President Clinton boasted of raising millions of dollars for early issue ads and personally vetting the campaign. The Republicans countered with their own spending spree, though they were slow off the mark, and soft money given to the parties reached $260 million that year.

Despite his boasts, the enforcers did nothing about Clinton, which had to mean they did not regard his actions as "coordination" that destroyed the "independence" of the expenditures. But if these actions were not "coordination," then nothing is, which means that the noncoordination requirement is dead. The FEC is now conducting a rulemaking proceeding to define *coordination*.

By 2000, Hillary Rodham Clinton's Senate campaign was telling people to make a big contribution and let the campaign staff break it down into hard money for the campaign, hard money for her related campaign committee, and soft money to be used by other committees for "party building." The president was equally overt,

---

> ### *The most conspicuous recent example of celebrity volunteering was Robin Williams' performance at the Democratic National Committee's record-breaking "barbecue bash" in late May, which raised $26.5 million.*

---

crisscrossing the nation to raise money from corporations and wealthy individuals, and the Republicans responded in kind, pulling out their own gate attractions, such as they are, and tapping into business executives and conservative entrepreneurs.

Celebrity Skin

The third gap in the law, though no reformer would dream of calling *this* a loophole, is voluntary activity by individuals, which is not covered by contribution limits. This exemption is an important reason for the rising political power of celebrities. The most conspicuous recent example of celebrity volunteering was Robin Williams' performance at the Democratic National Committee's record-breaking "barbecue bash" in late May, which raised $26.5 million. On a more modest but still impressive scale, an entertainer can contribute her time for a fund-raiser; draw, say, 10,000 people at $100 a pop; and net a cool $1 million for the campaign. The presumptively corrupting industrialist can contribute a mere $5,000. Politicians spend a lot of time in Hollywood these days.

Another important effect of allowing unlimited voluntary activity is to give power to unions and to big government, categories that are increasingly overlapping. About 1.7 million civilians work for the federal government, and almost 13 million more earn a living producing goods and services for the feds, not counting state and local workers paid with federal dollars. State and local governments employ 17 million people. Add it up, and 22 percent of the civilian labor force of 138 million people works for governments. Public sector employees are much more likely to be unionized than are private sector employees: Unions cover 60 percent of the direct federal work force and 38 percent of state and local employees, compared to less than 10 percent of the private sector work force. All told, about 40 percent of the nation's 16.2 million union members are public employees.

Wall Street Journal columnist Paul Gigot notes that "government has become the ultimate special-interest lobby, always arguing for more government and always in apocalyptic terms." The numbers bear him out. In the 1997-98 election cycle, the American Federation of State, County, and Municipal Employees (AFSCME) was number three on the list of PAC contributions, with $2.4 million, all to the Democrats. (Numbers one and two were the realtors and the trial lawyers.) Media references to the role of "unions" in campaigns are largely references to public employees, and under the current laws their power is considerable. Unions can establish PACs to give hard money, and they can use dues for soft money and issue advocacy. In theory, a worker has a right to object and get back the portion of his dues used for politics, but this right has been gutted by administrative and judicial actions.

Unions are also the infantry of elections. They get out the vote, go door-to-door, and stuff envelopes. In this year's New Hampshire primary, more than 2,000 federal employees worked for Al Gore. In New York, union members distributed 1 million Gore fliers at 10,000 workplaces just before the March primary.

Current discussions of "reform" focus primarily on soft money, but many reformers also want to control issue advocacy, since they regard it as unseemly for those with an interest in the outcome of elections to interfere. No one talks of tightening the rules governing voluntary activity.

Access Fees

A fair amount of support for control of soft money comes from businesses. Business gets a load of grief from the media for financing politicians, but from the perspective of the givers the system looks like extortion rather than bribery. They fear that failing to pony up means that telephone calls will be unanswered, submissions unread, and representatives left standing out in the hallway while deals are cut in the conference room. So, they think, why not go with the flow, join the public indignation, and encourage Congress to outlaw soft money?

Incumbents could easily be persuaded because soft money tends to go to the parties themselves, where the leadership can use it as a tool of party discipline. The parties could also use soft money to fund challenges to incumbents of the other party, or even to fund primary challenges to some of their own members. Democratic and Republican incumbents alike can agree on the urgent need to avoid such an outrage. Since a nonincumbent finds it impossible to raise significant hard money, soft money is the only real threat to permanent tenure.

Business people think they would still get to talk to their representatives without soft money, only they would no longer be required to pay for the privilege. They also would avoid endless time spent at fund-raisers eating insipid food and listening to even more insipid speeches. But it's a mystery why executives think they would prosper if campaigns were dominated by union (i.e., public employee) volunteers and the Washington media, and if no incumbent ever needed to worry about losing an election, not even the little bit they must worry now. (In 1998, 395 of 401 House members seeking re-election succeeded, a rate of nearly 99 percent.) If soft money contributions were banned, the realities would come home to them after a cycle or two, and the logic of the situation would dictate that the former soft money contributors would start funding more issue advocacy, conducted outside the political party structure.

What many "reformers" really fear is not the power of money but the power of ideas, especially ideas skeptical of government.

The federal government is now involved in every area of national life, and people with high stakes in government actions need to communicate about those actions. Those stakes need not be economic: Studies indicate that most campaign contributions are motivated by ideology, not financial interest, and those who think the government should go in a certain direction will wish to make their views known. Why would anyone think that candidates should have a monopoly on communications about themselves and their opponents, to the exclusion of interested outsiders? Only an incumbent could love this idea.

One can be sure that a ban on soft money would soon be followed by an escalation in reformist fire at the terrible "loophole" of issue advocacy, whereby those who care about political issues spend money on them. What many "reformers" really fear is not the power of money but the power of ideas, especially ideas skeptical of government. The true agenda is to suppress these; the corrupting influence of money is simply a convenient rationale.

Web of Regulations

Exhibit A for this conclusion is the reformers' attitude toward the Internet, which is becoming the newest "loophole." Instead of rejoicing that the new medium reduces the costs of communication and thus creates great opportunities to cut the tie between money and political speech, the FEC has tried to use the fact that it costs *some* money as a jurisdictional hook to limit it.

Four years ago, CompuServe wanted to create an "Election Connection '96" that would have offered free Web sites to all candidates. No, the FEC said; that would be an illegal corporate contribution.

In 1998 a Connecticut man named Leo Smith put up a Web site advocating the election of one candidate and the defeat of another in a congressional race. He argued this was not an expenditure because his marginal cost was zero. No, said the FEC; because the Web site was of value to the candidate, it counted as an expenditure and was subject to regulation.

A year later, the FEC was presented with a Web site called DNET (Democracy Net) designed by the League of Women Voters and another nonprofit entity to provide comprehensive information on elections. It decided this was *not* an expenditure and was therefore OK. But the commission did not simply repudiate its CompuServe opinion. Instead, it noted that it had considered a number of factors, and that "although all of these factors are relevant, different facts with respect to a particular factor may or may not lead to a conclusion that a website's activities are permissible." In other words, the FEC reserves the right to do whatever it pleases, without explanation.

The story does not end there, because the nonprofits then sold DNET for $30 million to a commercial operation, which is running it as *grassroots.com*, where it does many things that CompuServe and Leo Smith were forbidden to do. This has triggered a formal complaint to the FEC from the conservative National Legal and Policy Center, which wants to make sure the FEC does not give breaks to the politically correct that are not available to all.

In the meantime, the FEC, faced with a deluge of requests for clarification of its Internet policies, has punted. In December 1999 it issued a request for comment on all aspects of Internet use in campaigns. It received more than 1,200 responses (all of which can be read at *www.fec.gov/internet. html*) and is now digesting them. The word on the street is that the commission has no intention of doing anything before November, so everyone is left to speculate about what rules apply and what risks they face if they run afoul of what the FEC decides in the future. With any luck, the pressures of the Internet will trigger the demise of the whole system by making the FEC's efforts to micro-manage political speech patently impossible.

Real Reform

"That's not a bug," the computer joke goes, "it's a feature." So it is with campaign finance regulation. The loopholes are the only good part of the system. Instead of fretting about how to close them, we should be figuring out how we ever went down such a ridiculous path in the first place, and about how to inoculate the body politic against future folly.

The core idea that too much is spent on elections is downright silly. In 1995-96, federal elections cost about $11 per potential voter. The federal government that year spent about $1.7 trillion, which is about $8,600 per voter; indirectly allocated huge additional chunks of resources; and affected people's well-being in all sorts of other, noneconomic ways. And we are supposed to be appalled that educating the citizenry about the people we put in charge of these activities costs $11 per voter? Clearly, the problem is the reverse: There is gross underinvestment in political information, a problem exacerbated by the reform laws.

Instead of fretting about how to close [the loopholes], we should be figuring out how we ever went down such a ridiculous path in the first place.

Equally wrong-headed is the idea that most campaign contributions are motivated by a desire for favors. There is a real, though limited, problem with federal corporate welfare payments and associated unsavoriness, but on big issues contributions do not matter much. Business cannot buy votes on Social Security, or defense, or the minimum wage. Bradley A. Smith, a law professor at Capital University in Ohio and a shrewd scholar of the process, wrote in 1996: "Those who have studied voting patterns . . . are almost unanimous in finding that campaign contributions affect very few votes in the legislature. The primary factors in determining a legislator's votes are party affiliation, ideology, and constituent views and needs. That has been reflected in study after study over the past 20 years. . . . Donors contribute to candidates believed to favor their positions, not the other way round." (Smith, whose skepticism about current regulations scares the so-called reformers, was confirmed as a member of the FEC in May.)

The final rationale trotted out by the reformers is the "appearance of corruption." Even if the system is not really corrupt, people *think* it's corrupt, so the government (i.e., incumbents) should regulate it to avoid this appearance. Unfortunately, the Supreme Court has been sympathetic to this nonsense, which is odd because in every other area of First Amendment jurisprudence such arguments get the summary rejection they deserve.

A real program of campaign finance reform would start from the premise that the First Amendment is not, as the reformers seem to believe, a loophole. The First Amendment, as applied to electoral campaigns, is an indispensable element of representative government. The only real reform needed is to expand the loopholes, not end them. Contribution limits should be removed, even for corporations and unions, and the only requirement should be full and immediate disclosure over the Internet.

There can be First Amendment objections to disclosure, since anonymity is sometimes important. But contribution sources are important pieces of information for voters to get, disclosure is necessary for public acceptance of radical change, and it is a reasonable price to get rid of the present system. Beyond the disclosure requirement, let it rip. The more money spent, the better. The more voices, the better. The more that citizens feel they can participate and be heard, the better. The less governments try to control advocacy, the better.

It won't be pretty. There will be lots of abuses, problems, and outrages. But, as Winston Churchill said of democracy itself, this approach to campaign finance has one irrefutable argument in its favor: All the other systems are worse.

A Look At . . . Roadblocks to Campaign Reform[7]

By Milton S. Gwirtzman
Washington Post, January 12, 1997

The most formidable obstacle to campaign finance reform is not the politicians who depend upon the present sleazy system to get elected. It is the U.S. Supreme Court, whose members hold office for life. Unless the court is willing to change its view that campaign spending is the equivalent of free speech, any effective reform law is sure to be struck down as unconstitutional.

The first and last time Congress passed comprehensive campaign finance reform was in 1974, after large contributions to the Nixon campaign from corporate executives were used to sabotage opposition candidates and were found in the bank accounts of the Watergate burglars. The law limited contributions to $1,000 per person, per election. It set realistic ceilings on what candidates could spend from their own pockets and what others could spend on their behalf. It would have worked. But key parts of it were never allowed to go into effect. In a series of decisions flowing from *Buckley v. Valeo* in 1976, the Supreme Court used the free speech guarantee of the First Amendment to dismantle the law, piece by piece, until, as the last election showed, there are no effective restraints left on the amount of money that can be poured into campaigns. The *Buckley* case was an unusual one in that the court was being asked to render an advisory opinion on a law before it had a chance to work. The decision reads like the pronouncement of Plato's philosopher king on campaigns in an ideal world. But, as Justice Byron White warned in his dissent, the politicians who wrote the law knew much more about campaign reality than the court did.

The result has been a fundamental disconnect between the way Americans want campaigns to be conducted and the way they are actually run under what the court calls its "campaign finance jurisprudence." The court claims limits on campaign spending violate the First Amendment's free speech clause because they "reduce the number of issues discussed, the depth of their exploration and the size of the audience reached." But most campaigns do nothing of the sort. Candidates and their strategists spend most of their

---

7. Article by Milton S. Gwirtzman from *The Washington Post* October 30, 1997. Copyright © Milton S. Gwirtzman. Reprinted with permission.

money on television ads attacking the record of opponents and distorting their positions. Far from offering a thorough airing of the issues, the expensive ads concentrate on a few "hot button" ones presented in the shallowest and most simplistic way: "The Republicans are going to cut your Medicare!" "Bill Clinton gave us the largest tax increase in history!"

The court showed the same naivete when it gave the green light to the unlimited "independent expenditures" that were the source of such embarrassment in last year's presidential election. The court, having in mind the lone activist who prints fliers to hand out in the street, said this kind of spending "may well provide little assistance

---

> *Campaign debate is controlled by the candidates, who want to raise and spend as much as they think they need to get elected, and by their media consultants, who would like them to spend as much as possible.*

---

to the candidate's campaign." The court did not anticipate that interest groups and political parties would raise hundreds of millions of dollars outside the contribution limits and spend it to promote specific candidates.

The court has also been clueless about who controls modern campaigns. "In the free society ordained by our Constitution," it said in *Buckley*, "it is not the government but the people—individually as citizens and candidates and collectively as associations and political committees—who must retain control over the quantity and range" of political debate.

But the voters have little say in the matter. Campaign debate is controlled by the candidates, who want to raise and spend as much as they think they need to get elected, and by their media consultants, who would like them to spend as much as possible since their compensation depends upon the number of television spots they place. Ironically, when voters have tried to control the debate, by passing initiatives and referendums limiting campaign spending (nine states have done this, including six last year), the lower courts have struck them down as unconstitutional under *Buckley v. Valeo*.

The revulsion to this state of affairs has spread to every part of society, it seems, except for the judiciary. In poll after poll, by margins of up to 8 to 1, voters have said they want more limits on spending and contributions. After the last election, they told poll takers that the hundreds of millions spent between the conventions and

November had no effect on their ultimate votes, but that the way campaigns are paid for was a major reason for their lack of trust in public officials.

For their own part, scores of elected officials express frustration at how the constant begging for money saps their time, hurts their dignity and offends their sense of decency. As George Mitchell said on the floor of the Senate in 1993, after a third attempt to break a filibuster on a campaign reform bill had failed: "Mr. President, this system stinks. Every senator who participates in it knows it stinks. And the American people are right when they mistrust this system, when what matters most in seeking public office is not integrity, not ability, not judgment, not reason, not responsibility,

> *The best way to confront the court directly with the need for change is for Congress to reenact the spending limits the* Buckley *case found unconstitutional.*

not experience, not intelligence, but money. . . . Money dominates the system. Money infuses the system. Money is the system."

Just about every legal scholar in the field has criticized the court on campaign finance. Prof. Paul Freund of the Harvard Law School wrote: "Campaign contributors are operating vicariously through the power of their purse rather than through the power of their ideas. I would scale that relatively lower in the hierarchy of First Amendment values. Television ads have their value surely, and yet in terms of the philosophy of the First Amendment seem to be minimally the kind of speech or communication that is to be protected. We are dealing here not so much with the right of personal expression or even association, but with dollars and decibels. And just as the volume of sound may be limited by law so may the volume of dollars, without violating the First Amendment."

The best way to confront the court directly with the need for change is for Congress to reenact the spending limits the *Buckley* case found unconstitutional. To buttress its constitutionality, the law should begin with extensive findings of fact about the corrosive influence of the present system and firmly declare its purposes: to prevent corruption or the appearance of corruption; to enhance the quality of our system of democratic self-government; and to equalize the influence of all citizens in the political process, both as voters and active participants.

The limits themselves should be adjusted for inflation, as could the limit on contributions. This would mean a nominee for president could spend $60 million, someone running for the House could spend $210,000 (and an equal amount if there is a primary), and general election spending for a Senate campaign would be limited to 36 cents per eligible voter. This would limit Senate nominees to around $1.7 million in a mid-size state such as Massachusetts and $3.2 million in a large one such as Illinois.

These are reasonable amounts of money, far less than has been spent in recent years. (Each Massachusetts Senate candidate spent more than $7 million last year.)

What chance is there, if the current scandal goes deep enough and long enough to produce an effective bill like this, that the court will uphold it? In the past, when the court has reversed its decisions on broad public issues, it was because the previous doctrine was badly out of sync with the way American society now views its social and political requirements and, indeed, the fundamental principles of justice.

Brown v. Board of Education reversed the court's sanctioning of segregated schools. Until the Scottsboro Boys decision in 1932, the right to a fair trial in a criminal case did not necessarily include the right to obtain a lawyer. For most of our history, state legislative districts were rigged to give rural voters greater representation than city people. In its reapportionment decisions in 1962, the court forced state legislatures to redraw their districts so that every person's vote would have an equal weight. In reversing itself those times, the court had the sense and the courage to read the Constitution as a living document, whose interpretation could change with the changing perception of society's needs.

The members of the Supreme Court are intelligent people. They read the same newspapers and watch the same television news as the rest of us. I would be surprised if they were not as offended by what goes on in campaigns as we are. What they can do within the, limits of the Constitution is their responsibility. For the rest of us, the scandals of the 1996 election campaign offer a chance to revive the issue, and it behooves us to take it as far as we can.

The First Step in Campaign Finance Reform: Fix the FEC[8]

By Pat Choate
Intellectual Capital, May 21, 1998

Soft-money donations, unreported contributions and unwarranted privilege for special interests are not the chief problems in America's political system. Existing laws already deal with such abuses. Rather, the principal obstacle to honest elections is the calculated non-enforcement of those laws.

This non-enforcement, moreover, is neither an accident nor an oversight. When Congress created the Federal Election Commission (FEC) in 1974, it gave that new agency exclusive jurisdiction for civil enforcement of federal-campaign laws. However, it also structured the FEC charter in a way that keeps tight congressional control on this supposedly independent judicial body.

Through this cozy arrangement, our political leaders regulate themselves, maintain two-party control of our government, and limit independent or third-party participation in U.S. politics and governance.

Congress Controls Its Regulators

Political campaign reform consists of three separate, but equally important, elements: 1) the laws that define who can participate in U.S. elections, 2) the rules on raising, using and reporting campaign contributions and 3) the enforcement of those laws.

Today, enforcement is meaningless because Congress keeps the FEC under its tight control, and it does so in several ways.

Congress, for instance, selects the six FEC commissioners. In the early days of the agency, Congress directly appointed four of the six commissioners, the president two. But the Supreme Court ruled in 1976 that such congressional appointments were unconstitutional. Congress responded with legislation that put two ex-officio seats on the FEC—one for the clerk of the U.S. House and the other for the secretary of the Senate. The Supreme Court ruled in 1993 that this, too, was unconstitutional.

---

8. Article by Pat Choate from *Intellectual Capital* May 21, 1998. Copyright © *Intellectual Capital*. Reprinted with permission.

Despite these two constitutional setbacks, Congress created other means to control FEC appointments. By law, for instance, Congress confirms commissioners in pairs. In addition, one appointee must be a Democrat and the other a Republican. In practice, moreover, congressional leaders select the two nominees, send their names to the president (who then appoints them as a pair) and returns their nominations to the Senate for confirmation. Consequently, reliable party functionaries control the FEC—they always have and always will under the present structure.

Traditionally, whenever FEC action threatens one of the two major parties or one of their prominent personalities, the commissioners vote along party lines.

The commissioners' reward for their dependability is re-appointment to a job with a six-year term that pays more than $133,000 annually plus benefits. One of the five current FEC commissioners, for instance, has held office since 1975, and four others have been there since the early 1980s. The current FEC vacancy exists because a commissioner resigned to become a campaign-law consultant.

Congressional control, however, extends far beyond putting its own people on the commission. Federal campaign laws require, for example, that four of the six FEC commissioners must approve any investigation or any substantive act by FEC professional staff. Without a majority vote, therefore, the FEC general counsel cannot issue a subpoena and the FEC staff cannot initiate any compliance activities. In 1979, Congress also prohibited the FEC from making random audits of candidates, parties and political-action committees.

Traditionally, whenever FEC action threatens one of the two major parties or one of their prominent personalities, the commissioners vote along party lines. A tie vote creates a deadlock that forces the dismissal of any complaint.

Congress further limits FEC investigations by refusing to allocate adequate funding for basics such as lawyers, investigators and auditors.

In a final surreal twist, Congress prohibits the FEC from levying fines against campaign-law violators. Thus, the politicians the FEC regulates define the sentences the FEC can impose. Consequently, the FEC may only suggest a financial penalty. If the suggestion is unacceptable to the violator, the FEC then must negotiate with them. These negotiations often waste months of time. If the negotiations fail, the FEC can go to court but seldom does.

The FEC in Action

Given all these constraints, the FEC operates as one would expect. It acts slowly—very slowly—and then regularly dismisses dozens of its older, unresolved complaints as "stale." The commission dismissed the various complaints against House Speaker Newt Gingrich and GOPAC, his former political-action committee because "too much time had elapsed." Likewise, the FEC closed its money-laundering cases against convicted Democratic contributors Eugene and Nora Lum and convicted Rep. Jay Kim (R-CA) because "it would not be the most effective use of the commission's scarce resources."

Not surprisingly, the FEC never has audited either the Republican National Committee (RNC) or the Democratic National Committee (DNC). Yet a vast library of evidence suggests both parties have illegally laundered millions of dollars into their federal candidates' campaigns. By contrast, the FEC automatically and aggressively audits the campaigns of nearly all independent and third-party candidates—which, of course, it should.

The FEC even ignores clear violations of the law uncovered by its own professional staff. After FEC staff discovered that the 1992 Clinton campaign had unlawfully received $3.4 million in public funds, the FEC general counsel asked the commission to authorize a formal investigation. The commissioners responded with a straight, party-line, 3-3 vote.

When a group of private citizens then filed a complaint on the same matter, the FEC dismissed it. When the private group took the matter to federal court, the commission opposed their case because it said Congress empowered only the FEC to enforce federal campaign laws—which it refused to do.

In another case filed by the Perot-Choate '96 campaign, the FEC general counsel reported to the five sitting commissioners in early 1998 that the 1996 Clinton and Dole campaigns may have "knowingly accepted" prohibited in-kind contributions from the Commission on Presidential Debates. The FEC general counsel then sought authority to issue subpoenas directed to that commission, the Clinton and Dole campaigns, the RNC and the DNC. The FEC voted 5-0 to deny its general counsel's request, and then, ignored the findings of its own staff, officially ruling that there was no reason to believe that these groups had violated any law. Case dismissed.

What to Do

Congress is unlikely to surrender its control over the FEC. Nevertheless, even if by some political miracle it would, FEC reform would require a total makeover—authorizing legislation, operating procedures and key appointments.

Fortunately, a shorter path to reform exists. We must break the FEC's phony monopoly to enforce civil complaints on campaign-law violations—that is, for the courts to recognize that citizens have a choice to either take their complaints to the FEC or to federal court. Private actions in the courts would cost the public little, and the decisions are likely to be fairer and quicker. Real enforcement through private action, moreover, will quickly reduce the abuses that are destroying our political system.

IV. Steps Toward Reform

Editor's Introduction

The fourth and final section of this book focuses on recent efforts toward campaign finance reform, including steps taken by grassroots organizations at the state and local levels. As Congress moves slowly toward enacting reform measures, local groups of concerned citizens have taken matters into their own hands, a trend that many believe bodes well for the future of participatory democracy.

"Profiteering from Democracy," by Charles Lewis, the founder and executive director of the Center for Public Integrity, reports on a proposed regulation offering free airtime to political candidates that was blocked by broadcasters and members of Congress. According to Lewis, the media was unwilling to sacrifice advertising revenue, and many politicians feared the advantage that free airtime would afford challengers. This article examines the seldom discussed role of the media as an enormously powerful special interest group. In the second article, "Senate Approves Disclosure Measures," Helen Dewar reports on the approval by both the House of Representatives and the Senate of a bill requiring secretive organizations known as "527" groups to disclose their spending habits.

In "Taking Offense" Jonathan Cohn explores the behind the scenes battles over the second version of the campaign finance reform bill cosponsored by Senators John McCain and Russell Feingold. The article also chronicles the efforts of groups such as Public Campaign and Common Cause to rally support for local public financing legislation known as "clean elections" laws.

Next, *Rolling Stone* political correspondent William Greider comments on the growing number of states enacting clean elections laws, in "The Hard Fight Against Soft Money." Greider also discusses flaws in the clean elections system, as well as challenges to initial efforts to institute public financing. He points out that, in the past, monied interests have been better organized than grassroots organizations, and he reminds the reader that democracy falters when ordinary citizens are unwilling to involve themselves in the election process. In "Political Reform Comes from Communities," Ric Bainter and Paul Lhevine look at local efforts toward reform, such as public financing, free local TV time in Seattle, Washington, and the decision by some communities to lower contribution limits. This article demonstrates that some citizens are no longer willing to wait for Congress to enact campaign finance reform measures. Finally, "Clean Money in Maine" describes the success of public financing in that state, a significant step toward reform that has already allowed previously unknown independent candidates to gain access to the political process.

Profiteering from Democracy[1]

BY CHARLES LEWIS
THE CENTER FOR PUBLIC INTEGRITY, AUGUST 30, 2000

In his January 1998 State of the Union address, after decrying the campaign-fund-raising "arms race," President Clinton proposed a major new policy that would address a big part of the problem—the high cost of campaign commercials.

"I will formally request the Federal Communications Commission act to provide free or reduced-cost television time for candidates," the president said. "The airwaves are a public trust, and broadcasters also have to help us in this effort to strengthen our democracy."

Within 24 hours, Federal Communications Commission chairman William Kennard announced that the FCC would develop new rules governing political ads.

But days later, the powerful broadcast corporations and their Capitol Hill allies managed to halt this historic initiative. In the Senate, Commerce Committee Chairman John McCain, the Arizona Republican, and Conrad Burns, a Republican from Montana and the chairman of that panel's communications subcommittee, announced that they would legislatively block the FCC's free airtime initiative. "The FCC is clearly overstepping its authority here," McCain said.

In the House of Representatives, 17 Republicans, including Majority Whip Tom DeLay, Appropriations Chairman Bob Livingston, future House Speaker Dennis Hastert, and Billy Tauzin, chairman of the House Commerce Committee's telecommunications subcommittee, sent a blunt letter to Kennard. "Only Congress has the authority to write the laws of our nation, and only Congress has the authority to delegate to the Commission programming obligations by broadcasters," they wrote.

Ranking House Commerce Committee member John Dingell, the Michigan Democrat, also sent an opposing letter to Kennard. Faced with the very real threat that his agency's budget would be cut, Kennard had no choice but to retreat from the proposed rulemaking.

---

1. Article by Charles Lewis from *www.public-i.org*. Copyright © 2000 Center for Public Integrity. Reprinted with permission.

FCC, White House Flattened "Like Pancake"

It was a humiliating and metaphorical moment for the FCC. In a very public way, the agency and the White House had been flattened "like a pancake," recalls former FCC chairman Reed Hundt, Kennard's immediate predecessor. But the threat of a shrunken budget and a congressional backlash ("[T]he likes of which would not be pleasant to the Federal Communications Commission under any circumstances," was the way Livingston described it), caused the FCC to back down. Free airtime went from the fast track to the back burner.

Many politicians in power tend to fear free airtime for the leg up it would give to challengers. And more than that, free airtime for political candidates would affect the bottom line of a very important industry and Washington player—the media industry. It would cost broadcasters millions of dollars in lost advertising revenue. They were not about to allow a direct affront to their financial self-interest to become law.

Indeed, the media's success in handling the threat of free airtime for candidates is but one of a stack of proposals that media companies have flattened like pancakes in Congress and the White House in recent years. Which is why the media is widely regarded as perhaps the most powerful special interest today in Washington —not that you are likely to read, see or hear much about it in national news media stories.

Winning Friends the Old-Fashioned Way

How do media corporations win friends and influence people in our nation's capital? As the Center reports in its new study Off the Record, they do it the old-fashioned way, by using the time-honored techniques with which business interests routinely reap billions of dollars worth of subsidies, tax breaks, contracts and other favors. The media lobby vigorously. They give large donations to political campaigns. They take politicians and their staffs on junkets.

Lobbying: Since 1996, the 50 largest media companies and four of their trade associations have spent $111.3 million to lobby Congress and the executive branch of the government. The number of registered, media-related lobbyists has increased from 234 in 1996, the year the historic Telecommunication Act became law, to 284 lobbyists in 1999. And last year, the amount of money spent on lobbyists was $31.4 million, up 26.4 percent from the $24.8 million spent in 1996. By way of comparison, in 1998, when media firms spent $28.5 million lobbying, securities and investment firms spent $28 million, labor unions spent $23.7 million, and lawyers spent $19.1 million. The media wasn't the biggest lobbying interest (airlines spent $38.6 million, defense contractors $48.7 million, and electric utilities spent $63.7 million). But unlike the media, none of those interests has the power to determine what subjects are covered in the local paper or on the evening news.

Campaign contributions:. From 1993 to June 30 of this year, media corporations have given $75 million in campaign contributions to candidates for federal office and to the two major political parties, according to an analysis of data provided by the Center for Responsive Politics. The next president of the United States will have gotten to 1600 Pennsylvania Avenue with more than a million dollars in political donations from media interests; Vice President Al Gore has taken in $1.16 million, Texas Gov. George W. Bush has received $1.07 million.

The sitting member of Congress with the biggest haul in media money—including his presidential campaign—is Senate Commerce Committee chairman McCain, who has collected more than $685,000. Overall, the amount of campaign cash from the media industry is skyrocketing every election cycle, which is typical of political giving in general. For example, media corporations gave $18.9 million in 1997-1998, a 61 percent increase over the previous, 1993-1994 mid-term election cycle.

No media corporation lavishes more money on lobbyists or political campaigns than Time Warner. The media giant spent nearly $4.1 million for lobbying last year, and since 1993 has contributed $4.6 million to congressional and presidential candidates and the two political parties. The second heaviest media spender in Washington is Disney, which paid $3.3 million for lobbying and just under $4.1 million in political donations during the same periods of time. This is not a subject either company was eager to discuss. The Center's calls to Gerald Levin, chairman of Time Warner, and to Michael Eisner, chairman of Disney, were not returned. Nor would the CEOs of the other big media political spenders answer our questions: AT&T/Liberty Media (formerly Tele-Communications, Inc.) chairman John Malone, Viacom's Sumner Redstone, Seagram Co., Ltd.'s Edgar Bronfman, Ralph Roberts, chairman of the board of Comcast Corp., DreamWorks SKG's part-owner David Geffen, and News Corp., Ltd.'s chairman Rupert Murdoch.

Junkets: Since 1997, media companies have taken 118 members of Congress and their senior staff on 315 trips to meet with lobbyists and company executives to discuss legislation and the policy preferences of the industry. Lawmakers and their staffs have traveled near and far, to events as close as Alexandria, Va., and as far away as Taiwan. They've spoken at anniversaries of news organizations, gone fact-finding in Cape Town, South Africa, and toured movie studios. The cumulative cost of the trips was more than $455,000. The top three sponsors of these all-expense-paid jaunts were News Corp., the National Association of Broadcasters and the National Cable Television Association. No member of Congress traveled more frequently on the media industry's nickel than Billy Tauzin, the Louisiana Republican. He and his senior staff have been taken on 42 trips—one out of eight junkets the industry has lavished on Congress. In December 1999, Tauzin left with his wife, Cecile, on a six-day, $18,910 trip to Paris, sponsored by Time Warner and Instinet Corp., a subsidiary of the Reuters Group PLC, ostensibly for a conference there on e-commerce. Another member attending the same meeting, Rep. John E. Sweeney, R–N.Y., reported half the costs incurred by Tauzin, $7,445. Tauzin's wife and his son Michael have accompanied him on several industry-sponsored trips to Palm Springs, Calif.; New York and New Orleans.

The inter-meshing of public and private sectors has, of course, been an endemic problem in Washington for years.

Despite calls to his office and home, Tauzin declined to be interviewed. Andrew Schwartzman, a public-interest lawyer and director of the Media Access Project, who has been watching Tauzin for years, says he is not the least bit surprised about Tauzin's trips. "Billy Tauzin is an active, knowledgeable and involved member of Congress who spends a great deal of time on telecommunications issues," he says, "But unlike some other members, he is not the least bit embarrassed about accepting large quantities of their generosity. This is the Eddy Edwards, Huey Long kind of streak in these guys of wink, wink, 'I'm a rogue' . . . Billy just kind of revels in it."

The second most frequent flier in Congress courtesy of the media has been Thomas J. Bliley, the Republican who chairs the House Commerce Committee. Bliley and his staff have logged 19 junkets over the last three years. At the GOP convention in Philadelphia, Tauzin, who hopes to succeed chairman Bliley, hosted a Mardi Gras-style celebration, complete with floats from Louisiana. The $400,000 affair, heavily attended by lobbyists and pols, was underwritten by, among others, SBC Communications Inc., which owns cable properties; BellSouth Corp.; and Comsat Corp. Not to be outdone, Tauzin's rival for top job on Commerce, Michael Oxley, threw an American Bandstand-themed bash, complete with the show's host, Dick Clark, the day before. Oxley's dance party was paid for by contributions of up to $75,000 a pop from the likes of Comsat, Satellite SuperSkyway Alliance, and SBC Communications; the total cost was estimated in the $300,000 to $400,000 range.

The intermeshing of public and private sectors has, of course, been an endemic problem in Washington for years, and the social and professional interaction between the media business and the government that regulates it is, not surprisingly, quite extensive. For example, Podesta & Associates, also known as *Podesta.com*, is the outside lobbying firm representing the widest array of media behemoths. Since 1996, the company has received $1.5 million as the Washington representative for Viacom, Time Warner and NBC. It is headed by Tony Podesta, whose brother John happens to be the White House chief of staff. Twenty-three members of its staff of 33 formerly worked on Capitol Hill, for either party. One of them, Kimberley Fritts, is the daughter of the president of the National Association of Broadcasters.

NAB Thrives on Congressional Ties

No media organization spends more money lobbying or has more people covering Washington than the National Association of Broadcasters, which has spent $16.9 million to persuade government officials since 1996. NAB President Eddie Fritts was a college classmate and is a close friend of Senate Majority Leader Trent Lott, and on occasion this relationship has been immensely helpful to the broadcasters. There are 20 registered lobbyists at the NAB, seven of whom came through the revolving door from congressional staffs, the FCC and the Federal Trade Commission. Until recently, their ranks included Kimberly Tauzin, daughter of Billy Tauzin.

Media corporations have spared no expense in Washington, hiring all of the "usual suspects" kind of big-name lobbyists: former Republican Party chairman Haley Barbour (CBS); Patton Boggs' Tommy Boggs, son of long-deceased House Majority Leader Hale Boggs and U.S. Ambassador to the Vatican Lindy Boggs, and brother of ABC News correspondent Cokie Roberts, (National Cable Television Association; Magazine Publishers of America); former Reagan White House chief of staff Ken Duberstein (Comcast, National Cable TV Association, Time Warner); former Nixon White House aide Tom Korologos (Cox Communications Corporation); former Carter White House aide Anne Wexler (Comcast, Univision Communications Inc.); and former FCC chairman Richard Wiley (CBS). After all, from copyright issues to broadband access to media ownership rules, billions of dollars were at stake for the transforming media industry.

Former Republican Arizona Sen. Dennis DeConcini, now a partner at his own lobbying firm, said that during his time in Congress, media lobbyists were omnipresent. "I was lobbied a lot by media companies when I was in Congress," DeConcini, who left the Senate in 1995, said. "The 18 years I was there, there were very complex, sophisticated issues that demanded the time of professionals interested in this area."

Even the CEOs Lobby

Frequently, of course, corporate executives are directly involved in lobbying process, and media moguls are no different. In his recent memoir *You Say You Want a Revolution*, former FCC chairman Hundt recounts important conversations he had with Turner Broadcasting System, Inc., chairman and president (at the time) Ted Turner; QVC Network, Inc., chairman Barry Diller; TCI chairman John Malone; DreamWorks' executive Steven Spielberg; and Disney vice president (at the time) Michael Ovitz.

Hundt candidly describes the atmosphere of influence peddling at his agency. "I learned quickly that the volume of lobbying defined the major issues before the agency," he wrote. "A single company might send soldiers from its regiments to the Commission as many as 100 times, visit or phone the chairman on a dozen occasions, call some member of the chairman's staff perhaps daily. Congressional staffers made tens of thousands of telephone calls to the Commission staff. Congressmen wrote letters on behalf of different parties, up to 5,000 or more a year. Sometimes, when the members wanted a particular result, they phoned the commissioners to solicit votes as they might call each other on the Hill. Smart and well-financed lobbyists also ran media strategies to persuade the Commission to write rules in their favor. Industries might spend millions of dollars on television advertising to influence a handful of commissioners."

The nature of the media's political power remains fascinating to Hundt. "The media industry does not mobilize great numbers of voters and it actually is not comprised of America's largest, economically most important companies . . ." The media's significance and political clout, he argued, comes "from its near ubiquitous, pervasive power to completely alter the beliefs of every American." Members of Congress and presidential candidates, he believes, are afraid to take on the news media directly for fear that they will simply "disappear" from the TV or radio airwaves and from news columns.

Still, no single recent media issue more poignantly portrays the clash between public and private interest than the debate over free airtime for political candidates. In early 1998, before the president and FCC chairman made their rule-making move, the broadcast networks, ABC, CBS and NBC, were already targets of criticism. They were excoriated for reaping potentially billions of dollars in 1997, when Congress gave them—for free—their government-owned digital spectrum to use for the next generation of technology. There was a rising public clamor around the question, "Do broadcasters have public interest obligations anymore?"

Ads Will Net $600 Million

Against this backdrop, television stations and networks separately have been making a financial killing from political advertising. According to data collected by a firm called Competitive Media Reporting, local and national TV political advertising will earn broadcasters $600 million this year. In fact, income from political ads has been steadily rising for twenty years—from $90.6 million in 1980 to $498.9 million in 1998. In the first four months of this year, TV stations in the top 75 media markets took in $114 million for 151,000 commercials from the candidates alone.

At the same time, around the nation, news coverage of political candidates is becoming minuscule. For example, the Annenberg School of Communication at the University of Southern California discovered that, in the final three months of the 1998 California governor's race, local TV news on the subject comprised less than one-third of 1 percent of possible news time. In 1974, the amount of gubernatorial coverage in California was 10 times greater. Another USC Annenberg finding: The 19 top-rated TV stations in the top 11 markets broadcast, on average, only 39 seconds a night (from 5 p.m. to 11:30 p.m.) about political campaigns. Top stations in Philadelphia and Tampa averaged six seconds a night.

Television stations and networks separately have been making a financial killing from political advertising.

As Robert McChesney, a University of Illinois professor, wrote in Rich Media, Poor Democracy, "Broadcasters have little incentive to cover candidates, because it is in their interest to force them to purchase time to publicize their campaigns."

Recent research seems to bear this out. For example, in the New Jersey Senate primary, in which Jon Corzine spent more of his own money than any Senate candidate in U.S. history, local television stations in New York and Philadelphia made $21 million from political ads. The last two weeks of the campaign, citizens watching top Philadelphia and New York TV stations were 10 times more likely to see a campaign ad than a campaign news story.

Broadcasters, says Paul Taylor, founder and executive director of Alliance for Better Campaigns, "are profiteering from democracy." Since 1996, his group, co-chaired by former presidents Jimmy Carter and Gerald Ford and by former CBS News anchorman Walter Cronkite, has been calling for the networks and 1,300 TV stations to give at least five minutes of political news coverage a day during the last month before the 2000 election. So far, only 2 percent of the broadcasters have agreed.

The FCC still seems to hold some interest, as do a few members of Congress, who have included proposals requiring broadcasters to provide free airtime to political candidates in campaign finance reform measures in the current Congress. But industry lobbyists do not give an inch on any of them. In formal comments before the agency in March, the National Association of Broadcasters "respectfully submits that there is no lack of political news and information available for persons who have any interest in obtaining such information. Thus, a voluntary or mandatory requirement for broadcasters to offer additional free time for political candidates is unnecessary." The Radio and Television News Directors Association stated, "Proponents of mandatory airtime for political candidates would prefer that the FCC ignore altogether the First Amendment rights of broadcasters. They would have the Commission turn its back on political coverage decisions made by experienced, professional journalists."

Some newspaper editorials about the free airtime proposal have been curiously consistent with the extent of their ownership of broadcasting properties. *The Los Angeles Times*, with no TV stations, wrote supportively of the free airtime initiative. *The Chicago Tribune*, owned by the Tribune Co., which recently purchased the *Los Angeles Times* and Times Mirror, and also contributes to political candidates and parties and owns 19 TV stations, saw the issue differently.

The newspaper wrote in 1998, "It might be good if candidates didn't have to raise and spend so much money to finance broadcast ads. In that case, let Congress provide public funds to subsidize campaigns. If the public stands to gain from improved candidate access to the airwaves, the public ought to bear the cost." In other words, let the citizens pay for the ads they increasingly must watch.

$11 Million to Defeat Free-Airtime Bills

The dirty little secret is that from 1996 through 1998, the NAB and five media outlets—ABC, CBS, A.H. Belo Corp., Meredith Corp., and Cox Enterprises—cumulatively spent nearly $11 million to defeat a dozen campaign finance bills mandating free airtime for political candidates. One company lobbyist willing to talk to us was Jerry Hadenfeldt, who represents Meredith, owner of a dozen TV stations, 20 magazines, and publisher of more than 300 books. "Free political ads are basically picking the pockets of a select group, namely television broadcasters," he says, "They [candidates] already get the lowest available rates, and that's the way we believe it should stay."

Rep. Louise Slaughter, a New York Democrat, introduced one of the free airtime bills he opposed. She apparently did not realize the extent of the industry maneuverings against her. When told that $11 million had been spent lobbying against her bill and others like it, she said, "Oh, good Lord . . . It seems excessive to me. I am absolutely astonished. They paid $11 million to kill it? Well, it sure worked, didn't it?"

Senate Approves Disclosure Measure[2]

BY HELEN DEWAR
WASHINGTON POST, JUNE 30, 2000

The Senate yesterday gave final approval to legislation to force secretive tax-exempt groups to disclose their political spending and donors, ensuring enactment of the first new campaign finance restrictions in two decades.

The bill cleared both houses by big margins after Republican leaders decided to cut their losses and abandon their resistance. It now goes to President Clinton, who has said he will sign it.

The legislation would take effect immediately after being signed, meaning the groups, including one closely associated with House Majority Whip Tom DeLay (R–Tex.), would have to disband, reorganize or disclose details of their fund-raising and advocacy activities before the November elections.

"We have established some controls on a campaign finance system that is wildly and dangerously out of control," said Sen. Joseph I. Lieberman (D–Conn.), a cosponsor of the proposal.

The bill would close a legal loophole exploited by a growing number of both conservative and liberal groups to raise unlimited funds for political activities without disclosing any details of their operations or paying any taxes. Perhaps the best known example is Republicans for Clean Air, a group founded by supporters of George W. Bush, which ran ads attacking Arizona Sen. John McCain during the GOP presidential primaries.

The bill approved by both chambers would require these "527" groups, named for the section of the tax code that governs their activities, to disclose contributions of more than $200 and spending above $500 every three months, with another due just before elections. They would make their first report this year by mid-October.

But supporters expressed concern that House and Senate GOP leaders might delay transmission of the bill to the White House, giving the groups more time to raise money before having to disclose contributors.

---

2. Article by Helen Dewar from *Washington Post* June 30, 2000. Copyright © *Washington Post.* Reprinted with permission.

McCain, chief sponsor of the measure, warned that 'there would be delays in the functioning of the United States Senate"—polite senatorial language for massive legislative retaliation—if there is any foot-dragging.

A spokesman said that Speaker J. Dennis Hastert (R–Ill.) has already signed the necessary papers and sent them on to the Senate.

The 92 to 6 vote in the Senate yesterday and 385 to 39 vote in the House early Wednesday marked a breakthrough for reform forces.

But there were no signs of an immediate boost for the reformers' broader efforts to curb the influence of special interest money in politics.

Passage of the [campaign finance] bill "breaks the stranglehold that reform opponents have exercised in Congress for more than two decades."—reform advocate Fred Wertheimer

---

"Today indeed marks a seminal day in our battle to reform our electoral laws," said McCain, who made campaign finance reform a pillar of his recent presidential campaign.

A campaign finance bill was approved by Congress and vetoed by President George Bush in 1992, but none has been passed and signed into law since 1979, when disclosure rules were tightened. Supporters hailed the new disclosure measure for plugging a loophole before it became so big that it could not be fixed.

Passage of the bill "breaks the stranglehold that reform opponents have exercised in Congress for more than two decades," said Fred Wertheimer, a longtime advocate of tighter campaign finance laws.

But even the bill's strongest backers were quick to point out that it addresses only one specific problem and leaves bigger issues untouched, such as the unlimited "soft money" that flows into political parties from corporations, unions and wealthy individuals.

A bill to ban such contributions has twice passed the House but has been blocked by a Republican-led filibuster in the Senate.

The six senators who voted against the bill were all conservative Republicans, including Sen. Mitch McConnell (Ky.), who has led the opposition to recent campaign finance overhaul efforts and said he was concerned about the constitutionality of the disclosure legislation.

But McConnell, who is also chairman of the Senate Republicans' campaign committee, urged Republican colleagues to vote for the bill in order to avoid political attacks. The constitutional nuances are hard to explain in a campaign and "I do not think this is a spear worth falling on" only a few months before an election, McConnell said.

After the vote, McCain described this as "quite a remarkable statement," questioning how McConnell could urge colleagues to vote for something he regarded as unconstitutional. "The last time I checked we were obliged to uphold the Constitution," McCain said. McConnell said he discharged his constitutional obligation by voting against McCain's proposal. Besides, he said, "I'm a practical man."

McConnell also questioned whether many groups would be affected by the legislation and speculated that some may choose to reorganize under a different section of the tax code or challenge the law in courts.

Taking Offense[3]

By Jonathan Cohn
New Republic, November 29, 1999

During the week of October 12, as the Senate prepared for a final showdown on the McCain-Feingold campaign finance reform bill, Ellen Miller directed her organization, Public Campaign, to do what every other good-government group in town was doing: pressuring members of Congress. But, while the other reform groups were feverishly trying to assemble the votes to overcome a Senate filibuster, Public Campaign was pursuing a different agenda: torpedoing a compromise bill that was taking shape.

The compromise would have replaced the McCain-Feingold bill's outright ban on soft money donations with a cap of $60,000 while raising the existing limits on other types of donations. In Miller's mind, it would have given wealthy interests even more influence: "deform" instead of "reform," as she likes to say. So Public Campaign's lobbyists began circulating newspaper advertisements that the group was threatening to run in the hometown papers of senators who voted for the compromise. "Instead of listening to us," the ad text read, "Senator XXXXXX just voted to triple the amount individuals can give to a candidate. . . . That's not campaign finance reform. . . . Senator XXXXXXXX: Out of Touch With His Constituents." The compromise never materialized, and on October 19 McCain-Feingold died for the second year in a row.

It wasn't the first time Public Campaign has played hardball, or, for that matter, the first time the group's putative comrades in the reform movement were left grumbling about the famously obstreperous Miller and her band of troublemakers. Public Campaign's whole premise is that, when it comes to money in politics, only an aggressive, strident, sweeping approach to reform can work. Piecemeal solutions, they argue, aren't only bad policy; they'll never pass. It's a strange argument, considering that in politics compromise is usually a synonym for realpolitik. And it may well be right.

Public Campaign dedicates itself exclusively to a reform it calls the "Clean Money" plan. Under this plan, the government offers candidates full public financing—that is, money from the taxpayers—for their campaigns. In return, candidates agree not to raise private money. The idea is to get at the campaign finance problem

---

from the demand side. Instead of limiting the supply of money to candidates by regulating certain kinds of contributions or campaign spending—and then watching candidates figure out new ways around those barriers—Clean Money reduces the demand for money by simply giving it to candidates. It's far more comprehensive than anything Congress has contemplated in years.

Just about every pro-reform group supports some version of public financing. The question is how you get there. The strategy championed by campaign finance reform stalwarts like Common Cause has been to pursue incremental, supply-side reforms—on the theory that public financing is too difficult a sell with a public skeptical of big government. The premise of Public Campaign is exactly the opposite: that the only way to pass campaign finance reform is to bypass legislatures altogether (via the ballot initiative) or to bully lawmakers into submission. An inside game, they insist, can never work, because campaign finance reform is an unusual issue: it doesn't pit one Washington faction against another but the entire political establishment against those outside it. As a result, everything depends on grassroots pressure. If the compromises required to cobble together a congressional majority sap the reform issue of its public clarity, then legislators have no incentive to make any changes at all—which is exactly what happened with McCain-Feingold.

> *Public Campaign has begun giving out a "Golden Leash Award" for members of Congress who are in the pockets of special interests.*

At the national level, Public Campaign has steadfastly refused to lower its expectations, focusing on pummeling opponents of reform. While past efforts at reform have generally treated legislators with kid gloves—lest swing votes be lost—Public Campaign has begun giving out a "Golden Leash Award" for members of Congress who are in the pockets of special interests. At the state level, meanwhile, Public Campaign works with local groups to pass actual laws. Key to this effort has been the group's emphasis on how special interest money skews politics on bread-and-butter issues, a strategy that makes the normally staid topic of government reform resonate with people concerned about particular issues. ("Want Guns out of Our Schools?" asked one recent ad. "Get Gun Money out of Our Politics."

AND IT'S WORKING. Over the past four years, while Common Cause and other reform groups have continued their quixotic crusade for incremental reforms in Congress—each year proposing ever-more-minimalist measures, only to see them fail—"Clean Election" laws have passed in four states. And, while victory in the liberal New England havens of Maine, Vermont, and Massachusetts was perhaps to be expected, Public Campaign also eked out a narrow win in notoriously libertarian Arizona. It turns out that ordinary voters, even in conservative states, are a much easier sell than Beltway politicians.

Of course, passing these initiatives is merely a first step. To be parlayed into success nationally, the state laws must work as demonstrations. Here the evidence, although hardly definitive, is encouraging. Anti-reform groups such as the Chamber of Commerce have filed several lawsuits challenging the constitutionality of the measure. But, to date, not one suit has won (Clean Election's most recent victory came last week in Maine). Even the American Civil Liberties Union, whose absolutist reading of the First Amendment has long made it a thorn in the side of campaign finance reform efforts, recently signed on to Public Campaign's crusade.

More important, there's evidence that the Clean Election laws may actually be curbing fund-raising activity. In June, an *Arizona Republic* story, headlined "ALL'S QUIET ON LEGISLATIVE FUNDRAISING FRONT," chronicled a sudden drop in the number of fund-raisers being held for candidates running in the 2000 elections. Activity has since picked up, according to local operatives; but, in one of the first major tests of the law—the race for Arizona's Corporation Commission, a board with vast regulatory powers over the state's utilities and telecommunications industry—the four candidates for two open seats have indicated they will seek public funding under the Clean Money law.

None of this means the future of Clean Money is assured. Several court challenges remain, and there are still kinks in the laws that the states must work out. At some point, an extremist candidate will likely qualify for public funds. If the local equivalent of David Duke starts receiving taxpayer dollars to fund his campaign, voter attitudes might change quickly. And, at the national level, if the attacks on individual members of Congress don't either radically change its composition or shame moderates into backing comprehensive reform—a tall order—there will be no Clean Money laws coming out of Capitol Hill for a very long time. Public Campaign's is an all-or-nothing gambit, and on balance the odds still favor nothing. That sounds pretty unappealing, until you consider that nothing is pretty much what we have now.

The Hard Fight Against Soft Money[4]

By William Greider
Rolling Stone, June 26, 1997

If you haven't heard the news, money is still winning. Though each day more dirt tumbles forth about the disgraceful role of special-interest money in the 1996 elections, Congress has turned its back on campaign-finance reform. Many people will despair that anything can change, but it's important to remember this bit of history: All of the great American reform movements—from civil rights to child-labor laws—started far from Washington, D.C. In state legislatures and town halls, activists first pushed their bold experiments locally. Their energy and momentum eventually led to legislative action at the national level.

And it's happening again. An impressive grass-roots victory occurred last fall in Maine when voters approved, by a 56 to 44 percent margin, a statewide referendum establishing a "clean elections" option for their state government Candidates for governor or the legislature will now have a choice: Either rely on the usual private sources for money or accept only public financng and a spending ceiling for their campaigns. Since special-interest money might bury a "clean money" candidate, the Maine plan offers matching grants to help challengers keep up.

The same idea, with many variations, is now stimulating debate and optimism in at least 14 states, from Connecticut to Vermont to North Carolina to Oregon. "We have to surround them," says Ellen Miller, the executive director of Public Campaign, a new organization that's coordinating the charge. "As long as an inside strategy is played, we will get what we've always gotten."

"The level of distaste for Washington fund raising is very high right now," says Miles Rapoport, Connecticut's reform-minded secretary of state. "And that substantially enhances the public's desire for reform. What we need to do is get candidates off the treadmill of raising large-scale money from special interests—or at least make it possible for those who want to choose the alternative."

The Connecticut clean-money measure failed narrowly on its first assembly vote last month, but it will be back. "This issue will be with us for years," Rapoport promises, "because the surge of corporate money isn't going to get any better. Absent reform, it's going to get worse."

In North Carolina, the reform coalition does not have to turn to Washington for campaign scandals, since there are plenty right at home. The Institute for Southern Studies, in Durham, has discovered, for instance, that a mere 350 families and business associates give one-third of all the campaign money raised by North Carolina's politicians from both parties. Who are these public-spirited families? Industrialists, real-estate developers, agribusiness owners, oil millionaires, financial brokers, utilities executives and, of course, the lawyers who represent those interests.

The insiders (including, probably, Bill Clinton) assume that except for reform agitators, nobody really cares about the corrupting influence of campaign money.

"They really believe in democracy—*right*," snorts Pete MacDowell, coordinator for the North Carolina Alliance for Democracy. "They're investing in the political system, and they get an enormous return on their investment. The North Carolina banking industry for example, puts $1 million [each year] into lobbying and contributions, and it gets $54 million in a tax loophole." MacDowell knows that the legislative struggle will be long and arduous, but he is excited by the reform energies mobilizing across the South, where business interests have always dominated politics.

Washington yawns. The insiders (including, probably, Bill Clinton) assume that except for reform agitators, nobody really cares about the corrupting influence of campaign money. People figure that everyone takes it, so what's the point of fighting it? Republicans deride the public-financing remedy as "welfare for politicians," and many voters no doubt agree.

I have a hunch that the insiders are wrong this time, that public revulsion will deepen as we hear more about the fund-raising scandals swamping Bill Clinton and the Republicans. The real barrier to reform, I suspect, is the public's sense of utter resignation about politics accomplishing anything worthwhile for it.

If the clean-money campaign were to choose a national poster boy, he might be the retired Marine general who is now Florida's state comptroller. Bob Milligan overcame great odds in 1994 to defeat a long-entrenched Democratic incumbent whose campaigns were bankrolled by the very financial industry he was supposed to regulate. Floridians were fed up with banking scandals; Milligan promised to clean up the office. His candidacy seemed quixotic—until public financing arrived for a dramatic rescue.

"The special-interest groups are driving the train," Milligan says. "That's why public financing is so good. It helps people like myself who are interested in participating in public service but don't have any support base and, as a result, can't raise the funds."

At 64, Milligan seems to be a model of the citizen politician who wants to serve without making a career out of it. He retired from the Marine Corps, in 1991, as a three-star general and became active in Republican politics in his hometown of Panama City. In Florida, the savings-and-loan scandals of the 1980s included outrageous cases of looting by highflying bankers. Milligan figured that he could improve things by depoliticizing the comptroller's office.

"I found out pretty quick that I wasn't going to get any support from the financial industry," he says. "My opponent was very cozy with the industry he regulated, and one of my pledges was to try to separate myself from that. You'd have thought I was going to assassinate the pope."

Florida's system of partial public financing was enacted back in 1986 but, because of various legal challenges, didn't get activated until the 1994 election. The state provides matching funds to candidates, who must first raise a substantial threshold amount on their own from small contributors who give $250 or less. Candidates who opt out and rely solely on private contributions can exceed the spending limits, but their opponents will receive a dollar-for-dollar match from the state, up to a point. "It creates a disincentive for a nonparticipating candidate to exceed the limit," says Sally Spener, executive director of Florida Common Cause. "For every dollar you raise over the limit, you're giving a dollar to your opponent."

Bob Milligan was such an extreme underdog that he struggled even to raise the qualifying threshold of $100,000. His opponent, meanwhile, had $1.3 million to spend. "He was extraordinarily overconfident," Milligan recalls. "He gave me no chance at all. But neither did anybody else. That's why it was so hard to raise money.

The cause of public financing is generally promoted by Democratic progressives (formerly known as liberals), whose candidates are typically outspent by big-money Republicans. But Milligan's victory illustrates that conservative groups and Republican candidates might benefit as much or more. The key to qualifying for the public funds is grass-roots organizing—the ability to collect small contributions from a large number of people. In many locales, conservative groups like the Christian Coalition are far better prepared for that chore than liberals are.

The larger point is that public financing doesn't eliminate the power of corporations and other big donors, but at least it does give challenges a viable chance to enter the race and be heard. Since Republicans typically raise more campaign money than Democrats or independents, it's not surprising that Republicans are generally opposed to the idea of public subsidies for campaigning. So are the powerful economic interests that now dominate our politics. In Florida, there's a continuing effort under way to gut or repeal the new reform system.

Milligan, now the incumbent, understands the pressure all too well. "The perfect situation for me right now would be no public financing

> *Public financing doesn't eliminate the power of corporations and other big donors, but . . . it does give challenges a viable chance to enter the race and be heard.*

at all, because I'm in the driver's seat," he says. "A lot of my Republican friends don't like public financing, and they ask me why I support it. But I would be hypocritical if I didn't."

The first federal legislation enacted to curb the political influence of private money was the Corrupt Practices Act of 1907, a law championed by President Teddy Roosevelt after he was embarrassed by his own money scandals. The act flatly prohibited corporations from financing congressional and presidential candidates. Today, corporations are back at the same game—funneling money to both parties through various back channels and loopholes—and, ostensibly, it's legal.

Common Cause president Ann McBride, whose organization is conducting a drive called Project Independence to collect 1,776,000 petition signatures to demand congressional action, says, "In 1996 we had the most corrupt election since Watergate, and it struck a nerve with people. They desperately want reform; they want a government they can respect."

"What we've done is go back to 1907, which is a hell of a way to run a railroad," says Fred Wertheimer, the former president of Common Cause. "The only problem is, we don't appear to have a Teddy Roosevelt around now to do something about it."

Wertheimer, a leading reformer, helped to draft the 1974 campaign-financing law that followed the Watergate scandal. The central elements of that 1974 legislation are now in tatters, shredded by court decisions, regulatory compromises and political default.

In the early 1980s, congressional Democrats went after the business money big time—moving away from working-class constituencies and cozying up to Wall Street and other monied interests. Democratic presidential candidates did the same and, along the way pioneered some of the abuses that subverted the law.

The biggest of these is the so-called soft-money channel, which allows unlimited contributions to political parties from anyone—money supposedly intended for "party building" activities but channeled, with a wink, into electing candidates. By Wertheimer's reckoning, the breakthrough was led by Michael Dukakis, in 1988, despite his reputation as a liberal reformer. The two parties consumed about $50 million in soft money that year, Wertheimer calculates, and $84 million in 1992. Last year $236 million was pumped into the national elections.

"Both Clinton and the Republicans massively broke the law in 1996," Wertheimer charges, "because both the Democratic and Republican national committees were just totally pass-throughs for the presidential campaigns. It's on a scale we haven't seen since Watergate."

Though Common Cause has volunteers in all 50 states, it is still concentrating fire on Washington—pushing legislation that would eliminate the soft-money loophole and restore some meaning to the rules and limits that already exist in the law. "I don't believe—when you have the greatest campaign-finance scandal in our history—that it is the time to turn your back on Washington," Wertheimer says.

Still, there's a depressing message in these facts that most reformers don't wish to face: The long, tortuous history of legislating political reforms has been subverted again and again by the inexorable hydraulic force of private wealth on political levers. Sooner or later money finds a way.

Public financing, for instance, ought to enable many worthy challengers to run for office at state and federal levels. But partial pubic financing has been provided to presidential candidates for more than 20 years, and it hasn't cleaned up the political money system. The system, in fact, got much, much dirtier. The fundamental struggle of American democracy has always been a political contest between organized money and organized people. As history demonstrates, when citizens are actively mobilized, they can prevail. Right now, the money is winning.

While voters in Maine were enacting their clean-elections system last fall, voters in Arkansas passed a different kind of reform initiative. Among other things, it provides a modest tax credit to reimburse citizens who contribute money to politics ($50 for individuals; $100 for joint returns). The initiative was led by a national network of neighborhood organizations called ACORN; the Service Employees International Union Local 100; the New Party; and others. Their slogan was, "Take the big money out of Arkansas politics and put the people back in." The measure passed by 66 to 34 percent and, it turns out, got more votes in Arkansas than Bill Clinton did.

In the long run, I believe, measures like Arkansas' may have a greater impact on reviving American democracy, because they create the means for ordinary people—including the poor and working classes—to regain their political voice. Among many voters, there is a widespread feeling that challenging the entrenched powers is hopeless. People of modest means lack the resources—that is, money—to launch viable candidates or formulate their own agendas.

The Arkansas tax credit is designed to help people see real daylight ahead. It creates small-donor PACs that would let citizens aggregate their small contributions and support candidates—or even independent parties—of their own choosing. And it gives political organizations an incentive to switch their own focus from the big money to the little folks, because it makes it easier to raise funds at the grass roots.

Among many voters, there is a widespread feeling that challenging the entrenched powers is hopeless.

My own concept of political tax credits (outlined in my 1992 book, *Who Will Tell the People*) would make them even broader. People should be able to contribute money to almost any activity that they think of as "political" and still be eligible for the tax credit—the Boy Scouts or an environmental group or a church-led community project, or, if they choose, a candidate or political party. This would encourage citizens to rebuild civic organizations across a very broad front, restoring the vital fabric of communities that is now so damaged.

At present, the tax code makes fictitious distinctions that allow the wealthy, corporations and tax-exempt foundations to contribute to so-called "educational" projects like Washington think tanks and propaganda campaigns, which everyone knows are really about politics. My notion is that citizens should have the same right to influence the public agenda.

If Congress enacted a federal tax credit for political contributions, I would add one other proviso: People will be eligible only if they voted in the last election. That's another incentive for voters to reengage. In 1996, more than half of the people stayed home.

In the end, accountability will not be restored to our democracy unless there is an engaged citizenry willing to sustain a continuing dialogue with elected officials. That requires a complicated process of democracy—organizing collective voices for the many—that is far more difficult than finding clean-money candidates to serve in government. It puts the burden on the citizens themselves. It requires them to throw off their passivity and to create their own politics. Democracy is hard work in the best circumstances, and, right now, it is in trouble.

Political Reform Comes from Communities[5]

BY RIC BAINTER AND PAUL LHEVINE
NATIONAL CIVIC REVIEW, SPRING 1998

Crested Butte is a picturesque town of nine hundred residents, nestled in the Colorado Rocky Mountains. Known for its outstanding skiing and its quiet, laid-back lifestyle, few would suspect Crested Butte of being at the forefront of a national, progressive political reform movement.

Yet, in November 1997, the citizens of Crested Butte voted overwhelmingly to establish a system of voluntary spending limits for candidates running for town offices.[1] In reaction to a 1995 campaign for city council in which a candidate spent over $500, the city council of Crested Butte found the political will to seek a solution, drafted the proposal, and placed it on the ballot. The referendum, which passed with 79 percent of the vote, set voluntary campaign spending limits at $200 per election, indexed annually at 3 percent for inflation.

Crested Butte is one small example of a quiet political movement that is steadily building momentum across the country.[2] Dozens of communities around the country are enacting political reforms to reduce the influence of money in their local political campaigns.[3] Often, these local reforms are enacted by elected officials in cooperation and consultation with community leaders and reform advocates—a level of cooperation that is in stark contrast to state and national reform battles.

Elected city officials, who are closer to their constituents than are state and national officeholders, know that their friends and neighbors care very deeply about the democratic political process. When they believe they can make a difference, people eagerly seize the initiative and involve themselves in reforming the political process to reduce the influence of big campaign contributors and increase citizen participation.

From Texas to Pennsylvania, from Utah to Minnesota, America's communities are leapfrogging the national debate about campaign finance reform and building a movement that could eventually

5. Article by Ric Bainter and Paul Lhevine from *National Civic Review* Spring 1998. Copyright © 1998 *National Civic Review*. Reprinted with permission of Jossey-Bass, Inc., a subsidiary of John Wiley & Sons, Inc..

sweep aside the obstacles to national reform. At the state and national levels, those obstacles are erected by well-organized, well-financed, special-interest opposition. The ability to overcome that opposition with old-fashioned community organizing and citizen activism is strongest at the local level.

There are two striking contrasts between local campaign finance reform movements and efforts at the state and national levels. The first is the willingness of elected officials to embrace reform; the second is the relative lack of involvement of national reform advocates. In case after case, voters work in cooperation with elected officials to enact campaign finance reform for their community, with the confrontational prodding of advocates centered in Washington, D.C., conspicuously absent.

In cities across the country, citizens and local elected officials are engaged in the politics of their communities and are actively striv-

---

In cities across the country, citizens and local elected officials are engaged in the politics of their communities and are actively striving to make local politics work better.

---

ing to make local politics work better. But that should not surprise anyone who knows political history. Almost every major political movement in this country began at the local level and was later codified by Congress. From abolition of slavery to women's suffrage and civil rights, major social change has always begun in neighborhoods, cities, and counties. Federal lawsuits and senate filibusters have never stopped such a movement once it began. The drive for campaign finance reform, and for even broader democratic political reform, is on the cusp of becoming another major movement as we close this century and look toward the next.

There are currently forty-five local jurisdictions around the country that have enacted campaign finance reform for their own communities, and twenty-eight states with laws that control some aspect of local campaign financing. In just the last three years, the number of local reforms has doubled. This year, the National Civic League will work with reformers in at least a dozen more cities and counties[4] as they tackle the issue of local reform.

Innovative Reforms

Here are just a few examples of innovative campaign finance reforms implemented at the local level.

Free Local TV Time (Seattle, Wash.). While national political leaders resist the notion of giving candidates free access to the public airwaves, Seattle's Ethics and Elections Commission uses the municipal cable TV channel to introduce local candidates to the city's voters. Seattle's "Video Voter Guide" gives each candidate for municipal office three minutes to speak directly to citizens; it airs on a regular basis in the two weeks before the election. In addition to using its municipal cable channel, Seattle has also been successful in getting the guide on other commercial, public, and local-access channels; it makes the voter guide available to citizens through public libraries.

Seattle's work does not stop with the Video Voter Guide. The community takes innovative approaches to disseminating election information one step further by mailing a detailed voter pamphlet to every registered voter two weeks before an election. Seattle also leads most of the country in the development of free electronic access to candidates' campaign reports.[5] These activities are not surprising; the city has a long history of successful innovation in local elections and campaigns, including establishment of the nation's first local public financing system for campaigns in 1979.[6] Seattle continues to lead the way in campaign finance work and sets a clear example for others to follow.

Public Pressure (Chapel Hill, N.C.; Boulder, Colo.). Citizens in Chapel Hill and Boulder use systematic programs of public pressure to enforce voluntary limits on campaign contributions and spending. The program was first implemented in Chapel Hill in 1995 by members of the local Green Party and Sierra Club, who sought to raise public awareness about campaign financing in local campaigns. The citizen organizers also hoped that their efforts would draw attention to campaign finance reform efforts at the state and national levels.

In the absence of campaign finance reform legislation in Chapel Hill, a coalition of citizen organizations met and arrived at a consensus on contribution and spending limits appropriate for their community. Then they asked each candidate to abide by those limits. The success of the program relies on an aggressive public education campaign by the coalition to publicize the program, the candidates' agreement or refusal to participate, and the campaign contribution and spending reports field by the candidates.

Ten of the eighteen candidates for city council in Chapel Hill in 1995 accepted the pledge to limit their campaign fundraising and spending. Proponents of the plan considered it a moderate success in terms of its effect in restraining campaign spending and large contributions. However, it was enormously successful as an organizing and public education tool for proponents of reform. The coalition of citizen organizations utilized the voluntary pledge again in the 1997 Chapel Hill elections and continues to work for state and local legislation.

Boulder citizen activists modeled their voluntary pledge program after the one in Chapel Hill. Troubled by campaign spending in the special election of 1996 to fill a vacant council seat, citizen activists and some city council members initiated the effort. The winner in that race, a pro-development candidate, spent $45,000 to defeat a candidate backed by the environmental community. Typical spending in previous council campaigns had averaged $10,000-12,000. The coalition of citizen organizations, which included the League of Women Voters, the Sierra Club, Common Cause, and the Green Party, implemented their voluntary contribution and spending program for the 1997 municipal elections. Their goal was to educate the

---

In Richland, Washington, the city council sets a voluntary "reasonable maximum expenditure" limit for city council races

---

public and prevent recurrence of the free-spending special election, with an eye toward passing municipal campaign finance reform legislation in 1998.

Advertising Candidate Spending (Richland, Wash.). In Richland, Washington, the city council sets a voluntary "reasonable maximum expenditure" limit for city council races and requires the city clerk to monitor candidates' campaign spending.[7] Richland's ordinance requires the clerk to publish a display advertisement in a local paper identifying the candidate or candidates who have exceeded the limit, recognizing those who have stayed within the limit, and listing the total campaign spending for all candidates. The Richland ordinance requires placement of an ad once a week, from the time the candidate exceeds the limit and on through the election. Alta, Utah, recently adopted a similar ordinance[8] that includes a publication provision like that of the charter amendment adopted by Crested Butte voters last year.

Richland's ordinance is another attempt to use publicity and the popularity of campaign contribution and spending limits to reform campaign financing. But unlike the Chapel Hill model, Richland has codified its limits and is willing to use public funds and the authority of the city to inform its citizens about candidate compliance.

Creating a Conflict of Interest (Westminster, Colo.). Concerned about the appearance of influence peddling, the city council of Westminster, Colorado, asked the voters to pass a referendum in

1996[9] that takes a conflict-of-interest approach to the issue of campaign finance reform. The charter amendment, adopted by the voters with an overwhelming 70 percent of the vote, declares that contributions of more than $100 create a conflict between the interests of the contributor and the interests of the city. If a sitting council member has accepted a contribution over $100 as a candidate or while on the council, he or she must withdraw from any debate and is forbidden to vote on any issue that "benefits" the contributor. There has been very little experience with the law to date. However, city officials report a dramatic decline in contributions over $100 from city contractors and developers.

Time Limits on Political Fundraising (Little Rock, Ark.). In Little Rock, Arkansas, the city's board of directors recently passed an ordinance[10] limiting the time period in which local candidates can collect political contributions. Candidates in Little Rock can begin fundraising only on June 1 of an election year and must stop fundraising by December 1. After the election, candidates must return any remaining campaign funds to contributors or give those funds to a nonprofit organization of their choice. Little Rock adopted time limits on political fundraising after Arkansas voters had already imposed a $100 contribution limit for local candidates as a part of a statewide ballot initiative.

California's Proposition 208 also contains time limits on political fundraising.[11] For jurisdictions with less than one million population, fundraising is limited to six months. For jurisdictions of a million or more, the time limit is twelve months. Additionally, all candidates must stop fundraising ninety days after an election and can apply post-election fundraising only toward election-related debt. Opponents of campaign finance reform have challenged the Prop 208 time restrictions in federal court, along with most of the law's other provisions.

Public Financing (from Hawaii to New York). Several local governments have enacted comprehensive campaign finance reforms that include contribution limits and voluntary spending limits tied to public financing of campaigns. Tucson, New York City, Los Angeles, Long Beach, Austin (Texas), and four Hawaiian counties utilize public financing in different forms as an incentive for voluntary spending limits. The oldest example of local public financing is in Tucson, where qualifying candidates have received matching public funds to finance their campaigns since 1985.

These public financing systems require candidates to meet a threshold number of small campaign contributions in order to qualify for the public funds. Candidates must also pledge to abide by voluntary spending limits and limit the amount of personal wealth that they contribute to their own campaign as a condition of receiving public funds. In New York City, candidates who accept public funds must also agree to participate in candidate debates.

It is likely that more cities, especially larger ones, will consider public financing as they look for ways to limit campaign spending and reduce the influence of private money in the political process. Reformers in Minnesota's Twin Cities and in New York City are considering ballot initiatives to adopt full public financing in 1998 or 1999.

> *A rash of campaign finance reform activity occurred at the state level in 1994.*

Low Contribution Limits (Ft. Collins, Colo.). At $50, the City of Fort Collins, Colorado, has the lowest contribution limits in the country. The Fort Collins City Council originally enacted a $100 contribution limit in 1981. In 1986, the council decided to lower the limit to $50 in order to further combat corruption or the appearance of corruption in the local political process. No candidate or citizen in Fort Collins has challenged the $50 limit.

Washington, D.C., also flirted with low contribution limits in 1992 when voters passed a citizen initiative establishing $100 contribution limits for district-wide campaigns and $50 for ward races.[12] The Washington, D.C., ordinance, however, only survived through one election cycle before the U.S. District Court for the District of Columbia enjoined the law, finding it unlikely to pass constitutional muster because of the low limits.[13] Using the preliminary injunction and the prospect of a successful court challenge as political cover, the D.C. city council raised the limits back to the pre-1992 levels.[14] After the city council action, the federal district court dismissed the case as moot before reaching a final decision on the constitutionality of the contribution limits.

State Reform

A rash of campaign finance reform activity occurred at the state level in 1994, with passage of ballot initiatives in Missouri, Oregon, and Montana. In 1996, voters in Arkansas, California, Colorado, and Maine passed reform initiatives, and 1998 promises even more statewide ballot initiatives as many national reform advocates abandon efforts in Congress and turn their attention to statewide efforts. Some reform advocates are predicting at least five state ballot initiatives in 1998 modeled on the full public financing initiative passed by Maine voters in 1996.

The 1996 initiatives in California[15] and Arkansas[16] specifically set contribution limits for their local races. The California initiative also allows local governments to establish voluntary spending limits that do not exceed an amount equal to one dollar per registered voter. Contribution limits for candidates double in exchange for a candidate's acceptance of the voluntary spending limits. Opponents of campaign finance reform[17] have brought federal court challenges to both state initiatives.[18] An early district court decision in Arkansas has already upheld the $100 contribution limit for local candidates.

Pushing the Limits of *Buckley*

Several of the campaign finance reform approaches outlined above push the limits established in *Buckley v. Valeo*, the seminal campaign finance reform ruling by the U.S. Supreme Court in 1976.[19] Limiting the time in which candidates can raise funds, recusing elected officials from votes when contributions give rise to conflicts of interest, and advertising compliance or noncompliance with voluntary spending limits are all concepts that will force courts to reexamine the broad principles established for national candidates in *Buckley*.

Although legal challenges to state initiatives may settle some of those issues, local elections often give a completely different perspective on campaign financing than national or state practices do. A $50 or $100 contribution limit has a different impact on the elections in a small town than it would in a legislative race. One of the challenges for reformers in Arkansas and California is to highlight those differences, and to force courts to consider the constitutionality of the local limits separately from the state limits in the initiatives. Local reform advocates will have to wait to see what distinction, if any, the courts make between the limits imposed on local candidates and those imposed on legislative and statewide candidates.

But in many communities that enact reform, no one will ever challenge the laws in court because citizens and elected officials accept the collective decision of the community that dictates limits. For example, Albuquerque, New Mexico, passed mandatory spending limits with a strong majority in 1974. Although everyone knew that the limits were unconstitutional under the subsequent *Buckley* decision, every candidate for public office accepted them until September 1997 (when they were enjoined by a federal court). Legal advocates can and should use these accepted and unchallenged local campaign finance laws as examples of reform that promote democracy without undermining First Amendment rights.

As we move into the next century, local-level reforms help shape the First Amendment boundaries for campaign finance reform. The experiences of such cities as Fort Collins, Tucson, Richland, and Little Rock inform federal judges about the impact of campaign finance reform on the election process. The decisions that come from legal tests of the local innovations will guide future national reform efforts.

Conclusion

Local communities across the country are seizing the campaign finance reform initiative from Congress by passing innovative legislation to limit the influence of big money in local elections. The rapidly developing movement for local reform is in the best tradition of grassroots political activism. Local elected officials and active citizens are providing leadership examples for state and national politicians that will almost certainly lead to national reform. The legal and political lessons learned from successful local reforms efforts in places such as Richland, Alta, Tucson, and Little Rock will instruct future leaders and eventually shape national legislation.

For those who believe that campaign finance reform is only one piece of the reform puzzle, more fundamental political reform will only come after experimentation in the laboratories of local government. The use of local cable TV; Internet access to political information; voting by mail, Internet, or phone; and proportional representation are some of the reforms that are unlikely to come from Congress but are already being tested by local governments, where the leadership, political will, constituent support, and foresight exist to revitalize American democracy. Successful innovation at the local level brings a sense of hope and optimism to the political reform movement that seems lacking in Congress.

Notes

1. Town of Crested Butte, Question 2A (Voluntary Campaign Spending Limits for Mayor and Council) passed on Nov. 4, 1997, with 79 percent of the vote (389 in favor and 104 opposed).
2. California and Colorado lead the nation as the states with the largest number of municipalities that have enacted some form of campaign finance reform. In California, twenty-one cities have campaign finance measures that are stricter than the requirements imposed by that state's Proposition 208 of 1996. (For more information on Prop 208, see endnote 15.) In Colorado, where just over two million people (92 percent of the state's population) live in home-rule municipalities, eight cities and towns (including Crested Butte) have implemented campaign finance measures.

3. National Civic League. *National Report on Local Campaign Finance Reform: Preliminary Findings.* Denver, Colo.: National Civic League, New Politics Program, 1997.
4. They are Philadelphia; Akron; Boulder; Minneapolis and St. Paul; Salt Lake City; Cincinnati; Westchester County, N.Y.; Albuquerque; Chapel Hill, N.C.; Rolling Meadows, Ill.; and Missoula, Mont.
5. Seattle Ethics and Elections Commission (Carol Van Noy, executive director), 226 Municipal Bldg., 600 Fourth Ave., Seattle, WA 98104; tel. (206) 684-8577.
6. Seattle's history of campaign finance reform dates back to 1971, when there were campaign and contribution limits and an independent entity to enforce them. In 1973 disclosure laws were added, as was partial public financing in 1979. A statewide ballot initiative in 1992 prohibited use of public funds for campaigns. Seattle continues to have contribution limits for local races.
7. City of Richland (pop. 32,000), sect. 1.01.060 of the municipal code (Reasonable Maximum Expenditures).
8. Alta, Utah (pop. 400), An Ordinance Imposing Mandatory Campaign Finance Disclosure Requirements and Voluntary Campaign Spending and Contribution Limits, no. 1997-0-1.
9. Westminster's Conflict of Interest Charter Provision, sect. 5.12.1 (Conflicts Based on Prior Pecuniary Benefits). The entire section was added Nov. 5, 1996. Westminster (pop. 75,000) is a suburb of Denver.
10. Little Rock (pop. 176,000), An Ordinance to Create Time Frames to Solicit Campaign Contributions for Municipal Offices; and for Other Purposes, no. 17.408, adopted on Feb. 18, 1997.
11. California Political Reform Act of 1996, sect. 85305 (Restrictions on When Contributions Can Be Received).
12. Initiative 41 passed in 1992 with 65 percent of the vote, establishing election-cycle aggregate contribution limits.
13. For a study of the effects of Initiative 41 on the 1994 municipal elections, see Center for a New Democracy and the District of Columbia's Association of Community Organizations for Reform Now, "Initiative 41, Take 1: A Comparative Overview of District of Columbia Elections under the New Contribution Limits Law" (Feb. 1996).
14. Prior to 1992, limits were set at $2,000 for mayoral races, $1,500 for council chair, $1,000 for at-large seats, and $400 for ward races.

15. The California Political Reform Act of 1996 ("Prop 208") passed on Nov. 5, 1996, with 61.3 percent of the vote (5,716,349 in favor and 3,612,813 opposed).
16. Initiated Act Number One (1) of 1996 (The Campaign Contribution and Disclosure Act) passed on Nov. 5, 1996, with 66.6 percent of the vote (487,732 in favor and 244,267 opposed).
17. The first challenge to Prop 208 was filed by the Right to Life Committee. Since then, several other plaintiffs have joined the legal action. The Right to Life Committee has taken a leading role in other legal challenges to state reforms in Colorado, Maine, Arkansas, and Kentucky.
18. *Russell v. Burris and Citizens for Clean Government*, No. LR-C-97-0089, Oct. 3, 1997, U.S. Dist. Court (Eastern District Arkansas); *California Profile Council v. Scully*, No. CIV. S-96-1965 LKK/DAD (E.D.Cal., Jan. 7, 1998).
19. In *Buckley v. Valeo* (424 U.S. 1, 96 S.Ct. 612, 46 L.Ed.2d 659, 1976), the court held in a per curium opinion that limits on contributions are constitutionally justifiable in that they limit the "actuality and appearance of corruption resulting from large individual financial contributions." The court further held, however, that expenditure limitations were not justifiable in that they limited the quantity of campaign speech and thus restricted political expression "at the core of our electoral process and of the First Amendment freedoms." Justices Brennan, Stewart, and Powell were the only ones to join all portions of the opinion. Chief Justice Burger and justices Blackmun, Marshall, Rehnquist, and White each wrote separate opinions joining in part and dissenting in part with the opinion of the court. Justice Stevens did not take part in the case.

Clean Money in Maine[6]

By Marc Cooper
The Nation, May 29, 2000

Thirty-four-year-old wife, mother and small business woman Sue Hawes hardly seems to fit the standard profile of a serious state legislative candidate. A former social worker with a husband on disability and a small child, she has a fledgling Internet business that provides just enough income for her family to get by in this low-cost rural corner of the state. The household budget is so tight she can't afford health insurance.

She has few establishment contacts, and her outspoken populist politics would more likely alienate than lure the typical campaign underwriter—Hawes is a well-known community activist who fights for universal healthcare, a living wage and "corporate accountability;" her wrangling with developers and clearcutters recently won her an Activist of the Year award from the Northern Forest Alliance. So Hawes figures she might have been able to raise $1,000, at best, for a campaign that is likely to cost ten to fifteen times that amount.

But thanks to implementation of Maine's Clean Elections Act, Hawes, running unopposed in June's Democratic primary for a seat in the state House, will go on in November to pose a serious threat to her GOP rival—serious enough that she could win. And she'll do it all without having to raise five red cents from powerful special interests. Under the terms of the act, and because Hawes was able to gather minimal qualifying signatures, the State of Maine will provide her with as much as $12,000 in public funds to carry out her campaign—a generous amount for her small district of just a couple of thousand voters. In return, Hawes has pledged to "run clean": to raise no other outside funding and to put no personal money into her campaign. To qualify for the public funding, Hawes had to collect signatures from fifty registered voters in her district who were willing to write $5 checks—not to her but to the Maine Clean Election Fund. If she had run for state Senate she would have had to gather 150 qualifying checks and would have been eligible for nearly $40,000 in public funding. "No way I could

---

have done this without the Clean Elections law," Hawes says from across her dining-room table. "I'm totally free to spend all my time talking to voters about the issues."

Maine was the first state to pass comprehensive campaign finance reform with full public funding (since then, Vermont, Massachusetts and Arizona have adopted similar measures). Several years of diligent organizing by Northeast Action's Money and Politics Project, working closely with Maine's progressive Dirigo Alliance, culminated in the 1996 passage of the Clean Elections initiative, which won by a 56-44 margin. With this year's election cycle, Maine's law finally goes into effect. The result is a radical experiment in American electoral politics: 115 state legislative candidates, a full third of the total running, are running clean.

The Clean Elections Act is prying open a
traditionally narrow electoral process to a
whole pack of progressive, populist and
reform candidates who otherwise wouldn't
stand a prayer.

The new law is appealing to all types of candidates who, for myriad reasons, are tired of the relentless, traditional hunt for deep-pockets backers. They include incumbents and challengers, high-powered mainstream candidates as well as more grassroots insurgents and minor-party standard-bearers—and even some of the measure's most strident former opponents. Beverly Daggett, an incumbent Democratic legislator who was the lead plaintiff in an unsuccessful lawsuit against the Clean Elections law, is now enthusiastically accepting public funding for this year's run. So is Norm Ferguson, a Republican Senate incumbent who so vociferously opposed the initiative that he sponsored a failed bill to take the word "clean" out of the law. Now he sings the praises of public funding. "I found that people were pretty receptive," he says of his successful quest to gather the $5 seed contributions he needed to qualify for public funding.

But most important, the Clean Elections Act is prying open a traditionally narrow electoral process to a whole pack of progressive, populist and reform candidates who otherwise wouldn't stand a prayer. And for 39-year-old George Christie, one of the original strategists behind the state's clean-money reform, that's exactly the way it was supposed to work. "Lots of people get behind campaign finance reform because they want to clean up government, and that's great," says Christie, who now runs the Dirigo Alliance. "But I always looked at this as a means to open politics up more to average people and their concerns, and ultimately to win power for a more progressive politics. As we elect more clean-money candidates we can more quickly move on corporate accountability, a living wage, universal health insurance, democratic reform of education. Maine supposedly has a 'citizen legislature.' Now, we have a great crop of progressive candidates who have a chance to make it look much more like the citizenry and make it more responsive to the needs of working families."

Indeed, it's not just Sue Hawes who's pushing the electoral center of gravity leftward. Apart from four members of Maine's Green Independent Party running clean for the legislature, there are a few dozen publicly funded Democratic candidates who—freed from soliciting campaign contributions—are pushing the ideological envelope. "I'm absolutely on the left side of the party," says a smiling 32-year-old Kelly Ann Staples, a single mother scraping by on an Americorps grant who is running clean as a Democrat for the Statehouse. Like Hawes, and like a surprising number of other clean-money candidates, Staples puts universal healthcare at the top of her agenda. Like Hawes, she cannot afford health insurance for herself or her two children.

The clean-election law "opens up the process and opens up the dialogue," says another progressive Democratic House challenger, 47-year-old Shlomit Auciello. "I wouldn't have known where to even begin raising the money to run." She adds, "But now just running clean in itself gives me something to open up my discussion with voters. I start with campaign finance reform. And when I explain how I'm running, people get excited. I've got people voting for me now who haven't voted since 1982."

Hawes, Staples and Auciello all at least thought about running as Greens. Auciello is a former Green activist but became disenchanted with what she considered that party's inability to conduct serious organizing campaigns. Both Hawes and Staples have recently voted Green and have closer ties to that party than to the Democrats. Indeed, some Greenish candidates, now seeing electoral victory as a real possibility, have opted to improve their odds further by relying on the more solid infrastructure of the Democrats. "I would have preferred to run as a Green," says Hawes. "But they just don't have as big a support system as I will get from the Democrats: voter databases, volunteers and so on. It was a tough decision. But I went for the Democrats."

Hawes's dilemma, to go Green or Democrat, underlines the fact that while comprehensive campaign finance reform creates the possibility of enhanced insurgent campaigns (either inside or outside the Democratic Party), it is not, by itself, a silver bullet. For third-party efforts, there are also the inevitable ballot-access hurdles to overcome—not to mention voter consciousness. Take the case of the Green Party, which has twice run gubernatorial candidates who have won 6-9 percent of the vote. After the Clean Elections Act passed, the party put out an exuberant press release proclaiming that, thanks to public funding, it would now field candidates in some fifty of the state's 186 legislative districts.

But when qualifying deadlines for this election cycle expired in mid-March, there were only four Green candidates. Part of the problem was steep ballot-access rules that require House and Senate candidates to get twenty-five and 100 signatures, respectively, from registered voters within their own party and district (the signatures needed for clean money qualification can be from any party). "Getting 100 Green signatures was very tough for me, and I come from a part of the state where we have our highest numbers," says 29-year old Matt Scease, who is making a run for the Senate. One veteran Green strategist, who wants to stay anonymous, adds that the clean-elections process now confronts his party with as much of a challenge as an opportunity. "It's easy to always lose," he says. "But do we have the courage to assume responsibility for trying to win?"

Thanks to the clean-money law there are already more competitive primaries this year than there were two years ago.

The reformed process also confronts other potentially key progressive groups with new decisions. Organized labor in Maine, for example, has shown its willingness to stray from the Democratic establishment on occasion and support insurgents. But will it now, in targeted races where the Democrat is antilabor, support a publicly financed Green or other candidate who will have the money to run a serious campaign? Matt Scease's campaign will be an interesting test. His conservative GOP opponent has an abominable labor record. His Democratic rival is a mere ballot-line placeholder who will not seriously campaign. For the unions that represent the 7,600 workers at the historic Bath Iron Works in Scease's district, endorsing Scease should be a no-brainer. And yet, that labor support is still far from certain. "Too often we have argued that we need only reform the system and everything will fall into place," says the veteran Green organizer. "And we too often forget about that small thing called political consciousness."

Some potential candidates were wary about being guinea pigs for an untested system, but thanks to the clean-money law there are already more competitive primaries this year than there were two years ago. An even greater number of contenders is expected in 2002, in part because some initial polling indicates that clean candidates have a definite edge over "dirty" ones. Popular support for the system has also increased: A higher percentage of Maine citizens now check off a donation to the Clean Election Fund on their tax return than do those for the federal election fund.

Also in 2002, the clean-money law kicks in for the gubernatorial race, providing some $700,000 for qualifying candidates. Already, progressive groups like Dirigo are focusing on a short list of possible contenders. Says Green Senate candidate Scease, "We are going to need a lot of qualifying signatures. But what a great party-building tool it will be to dig out and sign up all those names. And how exciting it will be to see the playing field leveled out by Clean Elections. It's in the big, expensive gubernatorial race where you see the biggest money gap. A real challenge from us in 2002 could be the real political earthquake."

In the meantime, political reformers will be carefully assessing each tremor radiating out from Maine's new process. Already, unsuccessful court challenges brought by a strange coalition of antiabortion groups and the Maine Civil Liberties Union have set important national precedents. The federal courts upheld the principle that public funding could be given in exchange for not raising money from other sources. "More important, the court said it was fair to provide additional matching public funds when a clean-money candidate is outspent," says John Brautigam, executive director of the Maine Citizens Leadership Fund. "This is a crucial precedent for other states."

In the wake of John McCain's presidential primary campaign, the issue of campaign finance reform resonates more than ever. "We're excited by what's happening in Maine, because now Clean Money is no longer an abstraction," says Nick Nyhart, executive director of Public Campaign, the Washington, DC-based group spearheading clean-money reform. "And this is motivating people across the spectrum who believe in strengthening grassroots politics." He adds, "Our biggest challenge now is fanning the flames so that Congress starts feeling the heat."

This November, voters in Missouri and Oregon will vote on clean-money initiatives, and in both cases the initiatives are leading in the polls. In Connecticut a similar measure was recently approved by both houses of the legislature—an enormous achievement, given how hard it is to get incumbents to rewrite the rules of their own game—but the bill was vetoed by Governor John Rowland earlier this month. In North Carolina, statewide support for a pending clean-election bill is rapidly building.

Reformers are still confounded over how to get this issue to "break out" nationally and take root in large industrialized states in the Rust Belt or in big-money swamps like California. In the

March primary election, voters in that state rejected by a 2-to-1 margin a partial public-funding scheme proposed by conservative Ron Unz. Although it was supported by numerous liberals, including State Senator Tom Hayden, the Unz proposal fell far short of the sort of sweeping reform approved in Maine and suffered from severe internal campaign deficiencies. Now, Public Campaign is in the very earliest stages of exploring how the pieces of reform might be picked up in that crucial state.

"It's only a matter of time before the growth and excitement at the state level forces change in Congress," says Nyhart of Public Campaign. "The success of Maine and other states teaches us that we can win. And as the problem of money in politics keeps getting worse, we keep winning new allies to the cause."

Bibliography

Books

Anderson, Annelise, ed. *Political Money: Deregulating American Politics, Selected Writings on Campaign Finance Reform*. Stanford, CA: Hoover Institution Press, 2000.

Birnbaum, Jeffrey H. *The Money Men: The Real Story of Political Power in the USA*. New York: Times Books, 2000.

Corrado, Anthony. *Campaign Finance Reform (Beyond the Basics Series)*. Washington, D.C.: Century Foundation Press, 2000.

Corrado, Anthony, Thomas E. Mann, Daniel Ortiz, Trevor Potter, and Frank Sorauf, eds. *Campaign Finance Reform: A Sourcebook*. Washington, D.C.: Brookings Institution Press, 1997.

Dwyre, Dana, and Victoria Farrar-Myers. *Legislative Labyrinth: Congress and Campaign Finance Reform*. Washington, D.C.: Congressional Quarterly Books, 2000.

Gais, Thomas. *Improper Influence: Campaign Finance Law, Political Interest Groups, and the Problem of Equality*. Ann Arbor: University of Michigan Press, 1996.

Greider, William. *Who Will Tell the People: The Betrayal of American Democracy*. New York: Touchstone Books, 1993.

Kubiak, Greg D. *The Gilded Dome: The U.S. Senate and Campaign Finance Reform*. Norman, OK: University of Oklahoma Press, 1994.

Lewis, Charles, and the Center for Public Integrity. *The Buying of the President 2000*. New York: Avon Books, 2000.

Magleby, David B. and Candice J. Nelson. *The Money Chase: Congressional Campaign Finance Reform*. Washington, D.C.: Brookings Institution Press, 1990.

Nader, Ralph. *The Ralph Nader Reader*. New York: Seven Stories Press, 2000.

Thompson, Joel A., ed., and Gary F. Moncrief. *Campaign Finance in State Legislative Elections*. Washington, D.C.: Congressional Quarterly Books, 1997.

Timberg, Robert. *John McCain: An American Odyssey*. New York: Touchstone Books, 1999.

Web Sites on Campaign Finance

For those who wish to find more information online about campaign finance, this section lists various Web sites that may be of interest. These sites are only a small fraction of the many sites on the subject, but we hope they will serve as a good starting point. Due to the nature of the Internet, the continued existence of a site is never guaranteed, but at the time of this book's publication, all of these Internet addresses were in operation.

Alliance for Better Campaigns

www.bettercampaigns.org
A public interest group formed in 1998 that seeks to "improve elections by promoting realistic standards of campaign conduct."

American Civil Liberties Union

www.aclu.org
This site discusses an array of first amendment issues, including campaign finance reform.

American Prospect

www.prospect.org
American Prospect Magazine online features a special section on campaign finance reform.

Brennan Center for Justice

www.brennancenter.org
Inspired by former Supreme Court justice William J. Brennan, Jr., the Brennan Center for Justice at New York University School of Law works to find "innovative and practical solutions to intractable problems in the area of democracy and poverty."

Campaign Reform Project

www.campaignreform.org
A nonprofit, nonpartisan organization founded in 1995 by Jerome Kohlberg aimed at "revitalizing our democratic processes by working with the business community to achieve campaign finance reform."

The Cato Institute

www.cato.org
Founded in 1977, the Cato Institute seeks "to broaden the parameters of public policy debate to allow consideration of more options that are consistent with the traditional American principles of limited government, individual liberty, and peace."

The Center for Public Integrity

www.publicintegrity.org

A nonprofit, nonpartisan public interest watchdog group founded in 1990 to examine and review "public service, governmental accountability, and ethics-related issues."

Center for Responsive Politics

www.opensecrets.org

A nonprofit, nonpartisan research group based in Washington, D.C., that conducts computer-based research in order to track "money in politics, and its effect on elections and public policy."

Common Cause

www.commoncause.org

A nonpartisan citizens' lobbying group that supports "partial public financing of congressional election campaigns, ethics in government, and other aspects of money in politics."

The Electronic Policy Network

www.tap.epn.org

The Electronic Policy Network, *American Prospect* magazine's "consortium of top public policy organizations and advocacy groups," features a page on campaign finance reform on its "Issues in Depth" page.

The Federal Election Commission

www.fec.gov

The official site of the Federal Election Commission, featuring frequently updated information on campaign contributions.

Hoover Institution Public Policy Inquiry: Campaign Finance

www.campaignfinancesite.org

Founded in 1919 by Herbert Hoover, the Hoover Institution "seeks to secure and safeguard peace, improve the human condition, and limit government intrusion into the lives of individuals."

Public Campaign

www.publiccampaign.org

A nonprofit and nonpartisan organization dedicated to "taking special interest money out of America's elections."

Public Citizen

www.citizen.org

A nonprofit, nonpartisan, and member-supported public interest group founded by Ralph Nader in 1971.

Additional Periodical Articles with Abstracts

More information on Campaign Finance Reform can be found in the following articles. Readers who require a more comprehensive selection are advised to consult *Reader's Guide Abstracts* and other H.W. Wilson indexes.

Harder Than Soft Money. Robert Dreyfuss. *American Prospect* pp30-7 Jan./ Feb. 1998.

According to Dreyfuss, despite the continued growth of soft money, the most worrisome development of the 1996 election was the emergence of another and potentially far more devastating trend—the explosion of "issue advocacy" advertising. Individuals and independent groups with a favorite political issue are legally allowed to spend money on commercials, voter guides, and direct mail that yields public support for their causes. Money spent in this way, unlike soft money, does not have to be reported to the Federal Election Commission, and it does not flow through the political parties at all, but can be targeted at selected congressional campaigns. Most issue advocacy outlays during the 1996 campaign, which were barely disguised as efforts to place issues before the public eye, were de facto campaign contributions. The writer discusses aspects of this problem, including the watershed in U.S. politics that the explosion of issue advocacy spending represents; the bitter division among campaign finance reformers that the issue advocacy debate has caused; examples of issue advocacy in action; issue advocacy and the law; and whether Congress can find a solution to the problem.

Labor's Loss. Ellen S. Miller and Micah Sifry. *American Prospect* v. 11 p8 Aug. 14, 2000.

Miller and Sifry contend that the gap between corporate and labor financial contributions to election campaigns is expanding at a rapid rate but has gone relatively unnoticed in the 2000 election cycle. This is because the focus of attention is on the fact that Democrats have in some respects achieved parity with Republicans in the money chase, and everyone is concerned about the implications of this for the composition of the next Congress. Business consistently outspent Labor in the 1994, 1996, and 1998 election cycles in contributions to federal candidates and party committees. From the 1994 through the 1998 elections, the dollar amount of the gap between business and labor spending almost doubled, from $307 million to $606 million. In the 2000 election cycle so far, business is outspending labor by 15 to 1. The writers discuss the issues that are at stake as a result of this disparity and the fact that organized labor is beginning to understand that campaign finance reform is an urgent priority.

Reform School. Jonathan Cohn. *Mother Jones* v. 22 p62 June 1997.

According to Cohn, the current campaign-finance scandals offer the first chance in years to affect a meaningful reform of the system. The key campaign-finance issue is how to close the "soft money" loophole. A ban on soft money is central to the McCain-Feingold bill, bipartisan reform legislation that is currently struggling in Congress. The bill also seeks to limit out-of-state money in congressional races and would eliminate donations from PACs. Cohn suggests that more sweeping reforms, including a stronger Federal Election Commission, instantaneous electronic disclosure, and public financing, are also necessary.

Money 2000: The Election Will Break All Records, and We'll Lose. Robert Dreyfuss. *Nation* v. 269 pp11+ Oct. 18, 1999.

Dreyfuss comments that as America's national elections in 2000 may break all records in terms of campaign spending, the likelihood of campaign finance reform is diminishing. The Federal Election Commission, which at least modestly regulated the old finance system, will have no say in 2000. Instead, a freewheeling, open-market political system in which politicians and parties are bought and sold by America's elite will dictate proceedings. Genuine reform of the campaign finance system will require a political movement that is prepared to take some political power from the wealthy corporate elite. This is not something that appeals to the majority of Democrats and Republicans, or even some groups that support reform.

The Supreme Court and Campaign Finance. David Cole. *Nation* v. 269 p14 Oct. 18, 1999.

The writer discusses how the Supreme Court's 1976 decision in *Buckley v. Valeo* has proved to be the bugbear of campaign finance reform. In its ruling, the Court equated money and speech, and consequently it subjected restrictions on campaign finance to strict First Amendment analysis, rendering many attempts at reform unconstitutional.

Talk Is Cheap. Jeffrey Rosen. *New Republic* v. 222 pp20-2 Feb. 14, 2000.

Rosen discusses the recent Supreme Court ruling in *Nixon v. Shrink Missouri Government PAC*, which clears the way for more regulation of the campaign finance system, ignores the implications of the Internet, Rosen writes. The Court ruled that state limits on contributions were constitutional, and the six justices signaled their readiness to uphold even tighter restrictions. Nonetheless, the reality is that the Internet has made campaign finance regulation impossible: If Congress and the states ever imposed rigid limits on soft and hard money, wealthy donors would simply use their money in areas that received the highest First Amendment protection, such as cable television and Internet publishing. Technology has removed the borderlines between publishers, independent advocacy groups, and corporate donors, so campaign spending cannot be regulated without severely altering the Constitution.

A $3 Billion Record, But Does Anyone Care? Don Van Natta Jr. *New York Times* sec. IV p4 Jan. 23, 2000.

Van Natta, Jr. reports political operatives and campaign finance experts estimate that the 2000 elections for president and Congress will end up costing a total of $3 billion, if the current dizzying pace of fund-raising continues. The total in 1996 was $2.1 billion. Political analysts note that this year's front-loaded presidential primary schedule will clear the calendar to provide even more time to raise money. There appears to be no stopping the ballooning campaign finance bubble, but the issue appears to generate only modest outrage among voters.

The Maine Chance. Ruth Conniff. *The Progressive* v. 64 pp12-13 July 2000.

Conniff writes that after ten years of organizing, campaigning, and battling in court, Maine has introduced publicly funded political campaigns. A three-year legal challenge on the basis of free speech by the National Right to Life Committee and the ACLU recently failed, and 115 candidates for state office will take advantage of public funding in the fall. The voluntary system has given rise to a new generation of candidates who are not wealthy or who do not have contacts they can tap for big contributions. In addition, if a candidate refuses to participate, his clean-money opponent receives twice as much public funding. Not taking part in the clean-elections system has convinced about half of the candidates for state office to run clean, and advocates hope this will diminish the power of large corporations that exercise unseemly influence over Maine's legislature. Vermont's stricter campaign finance reform law is also discussed.

Buying Influence. Carolyn Hirschman. *Telephony* v. 238 pp66-7 Feb. 14, 2000.

According to Hirschman, telecommunications companies are contributing to both the likely party nominees and the likely losers in the 2000 presidential election, as both have a significant control over the industry in Congress. According to a January 2000 online newsletter by Public Campaign, a Washington-based campaign finance reform group, the communications and electronics industries have become leading forces in "efforts to buy access and influence." Although Democratic candidates Al Gore and Bill Bradley do not take money from political action committees (PACs), they do accept donations from individuals—including rich telecom executives. Moreover, even runners-up in the presidential race are receiving plenty of money from the telecommunications industry, with industry PACs and employees donating $122,738 to Senator John McCain, R-Ariz.—who heads the Senate Commerce Committee that influences much telecommunications legislation. According to Holly Bailey, a researcher at the Center for Responsive Politics, telecommunications companies are betting on the candidate they think will help them best in the future.

Clean Money, Clean Elections. Micah L. Sifry. *Tikkun* v. 15 pp45-8 May/June 2000.

Sifry claims that Clean Money reform enables a much wider range of candidates and voices to be heard in American elections. Most people understand the necessity of removing big money from politics, and this gateway reform will make other reforms more possible. The growing success of the Clean Money movement at the state level illustrates that the public is more engaged by sweeping proposals that offer comprehensive reform than it is by piecemeal approaches dependent on legislative compromise and backroom dealing. Furthermore, since real campaign finance reform is an issue that threatens the entire incumbent class and its wealthy special-interest allies, engaging the public at a grassroots level is the only way to win this battle.

When Does Money Matter? Adam Zagorin and John F. Dickerson. *Time* v. 155 p252 Jan. 17, 2000.

Zagorin and Dickerson report that campaign-finance reform advocate John McCain is being asked to explain why he wrote letters to various federal agencies in support of 15 of his top campaign donors. Shortly after Paxson Communications, one of the largest broadcast groups in America, gave and helped raise $20,000 for the McCain campaign, the senator asked the FCC to vote quickly on whether to allow the company to acquire a Pittsburgh, Pennsylvania, television license. In an attempt to prove that McCain also helped a wide variety of others, including non-donors, his campaign team released more than 1,500 pages of letters he wrote as chairman of the Senate Commerce Committee to agencies under his jurisdiction. In the case of Paxson, the senator's defenders say that he was acting in accordance with his long-term belief that federal agencies should not interfere in the free market.

The Money Jungle. Gloria Borger. *U.S. News & World Report* v. 128 p31 June 19, 2000.

Borger writes that, while Republican presidential candidate George W. Bush and Democratic rival Al Gore have pledged to reform the campaign finance system, they have already collected approximately double the amount of unregulated "soft money" raised by nominees in the 1996 election. Gore recently ran his first soft money ad, prompting criticism from Bush, who then proceeded to release his own ads. A loophole in Section 527 of the tax code allows special-interest groups to avoid campaign laws by claiming that they do not support a specific candidate. This has enabled donors to secretly give unlimited amounts to political campaigns. Ads funded by these donors supporting both Bush and Gore are discussed.

No Shame and Lots to Gain. Kenneth T. Walsh. *U.S. News & World Report* v. 122 pp32-4 Mar. 3, 1997.

Walsh writes that despite talk of reform, campaign money is still flowing into the coffers of both major parties and their candidates. Even as he denounces the system, President Bill Clinton is planning at least six major fund-raisers for the Democratic Party in the coming two months, and the GOP is mixing money, politics, and access just as vigorously. Political scientist William Galston, a senior adviser to Clinton in his first term, believes the system is gradually eroding the bonds of public trust and confidence. According to a new Roper poll, for example, 68 percent of voters believe politics is more influenced by special-interest money today than 20 years ago, and 57 percent say the federal government is really controlled by lobbyists and special interests. This cynicism is bound to intensify as investigators from Congress, the Justice Department, and the news media examine fund-raising abuses during the 1996 campaign.

Why Mitch McConnell Should Know Better. Michelle Cottle. *Washington Monthly* v. 29 pp9-13 Oct. 1997.

In light of Senator Mitch McConnell's vehement opposition to campaign-finance reform, the writer discusses a past political finance scandal in McConnell's home state of Kentucky. Investigations into the scandal began in 1990 when an angry businessman informed the FBI that Kentucky lawmakers were accepting money from horse racing interests in return for legislative favors. The case was closed five years later, after 21 indictments—15 former and sitting Kentucky legislators were found to be involved, as well as the governor's nephew, Kentucky's top lobbyist, and the Jockeys' Guild. Charges included extortion, racketeering, and lying to the FBI. In the course of the investigation, other shady dealings were uncovered throughout the legislature. Cottle comments that under such circumstances, McConnell's insistence that legislators are above contamination by financial matters is absurd.

FEC Admits Failures in Plea for Funding; Agency Outlines Wide Probe of '96 Campaign. Bill McAllister. *Washington Post* pA1 Jan. 31, 1997.

FEC officials told Congress that the agency needs to probe fund-raising among nonresident foreign nationals, the questionable use of "soft money" donations to political party organizations, party coordination of ostensibly independent political expenditures, and the "massive" but unreported spending on "issue advertisements" by labor and business groups. The FEC's unusual admission came as officials pleaded for more money for an agency that long has been scorned as a "toothless tiger," unwilling and unable to aggressively enforce the country's campaign finance laws. The FEC typically works in secrecy and does not discuss pending investigations. Faced with widespread accounts of the wholesale flouting of election laws, Joan D. Aikens, the commission's vice chairman, described an agency in serious trouble and unable to respond quickly to complaints and promptly fine violators. "The commissioners all feel it is taking too long to deal with these matters," Aikens said when asked about the FEC's tarnished reputation.

Tobacco Industry Said to Spend Millions on Lobbying Campaign. Saundra Torry. *Washington Post* pA2 Dec. 20, 1997.

The tobacco industry, preparing to do battle over a proposed national settlement with opponents, spent $15.8 million employing 186 different lobbyists to press its views on tobacco-related issues in the first half of 1997, according to a study by Public Citizen, a consumer group founded by Ralph Nader. Public Citizen, which opposes the $368.5 billion tobacco deal, said the companies and industry lobbying organizations used 37 in-house representatives and 149 outside lawyers and lobbyists in that period—"unleashing more than one lobbyist for every three members of Congress." More than $9.4 million of that amount was spent on the outside lobbyists, as Public Citizen found by culling through lobby fee disclosures filed in Congress.

Index